NOTHING *to* PROVE NOTHING *to* EARN

MOODY PUBLISHERS
WOMEN
BIBLE STUDIES

6 **CHOICES** TO LIVE FREE FROM
STRIVING & PERFORMANCE

NOTHING *to* PROVE

NOTHING *to* EARN

A SIX-WEEK BIBLE STUDY

BRITTANY SALMON

MOODY PUBLISHERS
CHICAGO

All emphasis in Scripture has been added.

Edited by Amanda Cleary Eastep
Cover design: Kaylee Lockenour Dunn
Interior Design: Puckett Smartt

ISBN: 978-0-8024-7154-3

Originally delivered by fleets of horse-drawn wagons, the affordable paperbacks from D. L. Moody's publishing house resourced the church and served everyday people. Now, after more than 125 years of publishing and ministry, Moody Publishers' mission remains the same—even if our delivery systems have changed a bit. For more information on other books (and resources) created from a biblical perspective, go to www.moodypublishers.com or write to:

Moody Publishers
820 N. LaSalle Boulevard
Chicago, IL 60610

1 3 5 7 9 10 8 6 4 2

Printed in Colombia

For the women of my childhood church: Pathway Baptist Church.
You loved me so well as a child and have always provided faithful examples
of what it means to be a woman so deeply rooted in Christ.
This Bible study was written in honor of you and the faithful women
of every local church who are doing their best to live *free*
from striving and performance, chasing after Jesus
with nothing to prove and nothing to earn.

Contents

A Note from Brittany

I'M A STRIVER.

(Probably not the opening line you'd expect from a Bible study like this.)

But it's true. I'm a hustler, a go-getter, and I find a lot of my worth in "doing things for Jesus." Some might even call me a little bit extra (my brother would call me a lotta bit extra). But the point is, from my early adult years, I hustled like I had something to prove because I did. And while friends and family applauded my efforts, since much of what I was doing had the appearance of good, with every new accomplishment, I felt the need to do more.

The thing about hustling is that although it might be socially acceptable, it's a real problem when you belong to a faith where our entire foundation is built on being saved by grace through faith! Salvation in Christ isn't achieved by any works that we've done, but through the power of the cross.

I've wrestled with this for years; so much so that I've spent hours in prayer and godly counsel, asking the Lord to help me truly find freedom and rest in Him. And yet, I still find myself coming back to the same struggle of trying to do the most for Jesus.

But that's not what He's asked of me.

The truth is, because of Jesus, I have nothing to prove and nothing to earn. Because of His saving work on the cross, you and I get to live free from striving and performance.

Amen? Amen.

Whether we realize or not, every day we're given opportunities to choose to rest in our identity in Christ or work to earn some sort of favor or standing. One of those ways leads to life and freedom, and the other leads to the bondage of trying to hit an ever-moving target.

I've identified six choices that we are already making that can lead to either freedom or further bondage. And each week we will wrestle with one of these choices:

Relationship vs. Religion

Character vs. Charisma

Service vs. Stages

Community vs. Isolation

Gratitude vs. Grumbling

Rooted vs. Restless

Over the next six weeks, we're going to be primarily walking through the Pauline epistles (letters from the apostle Paul), with a strong focus on Colossians. We'll be looking at Jesus and remembering that we have nothing to prove, nothing to earn because of His life, death, and resurrection. And we're going to wrestle with these choices that help free us from a life centered on striving and performance and instead offer us true life and life abundantly.

I'm writing as a fellow journeyer, one who wants to love God with my whole heart, soul, and mind. And I want that for you as well. My prayer is that you find safety on these pages to be honest with yourself and your Maker, knowing that He is good, He is for you, and He is inviting you to freedom.

I'm so glad you're here. I've spent countless hours praying over you and every woman who will open these pages. And I'm hopeful for what the Lord is going to do in our time together. So, without further ado, grab your favorite pen and a soft blanket, curl up in your most comfortable spot in your home, and let's start this journey together.

Brittany

How to Use This Study

Whether you choose to do this study with a group of women or by yourself, my prayer is that you'll open this book expectantly, looking for God to move in your life.

Because this is a thematic (or topical) study, we'll be focusing on a theme instead of walking through a particular book of the Bible verse by verse. We'll spend the majority of our time in the Pauline epistles, specifically the book of Colossians. But many of Paul's letters discuss similar themes and ideas, so we'll also be exploring Philippians and Galatians as well! In addition, there will be days when we learn from Jesus' life and parables in the gospels.

Each week we will set aside one day to examine the book of Colossians, and by the end of the study you'll have read the entire book. I've included a brief overview of Colossians in the following pages that will provide more context for your study.

Weekly Road Map for the Journey

Whenever I start a new study, I like to know where we're going and how to get there—a road map of sorts. This study is six weeks long and has five days of work with two days off each week. In the next section, you'll be given the opportunity to choose the type of journey you want to take and adapt it for your specific context and season.

Below is a sample of how each of the five days is structured: big picture, deep dive, reflection and application.

Day 1: Big Picture Introduction

The first day of every week will be light on content and heavy on Scripture. It's the day you'll read that week's Scripture passages and spend time observing and making notes about the text. On Day 1, you'll answer the same three questions each week that will help you start noticing big picture themes as you read:

- What does this passage show me about God?
- What does this passage show me about this world or humanity?
- Does this passage have anything in it that should be applied to my life, or that serves as a guide for the Christian life?

After answering those three questions, you'll have one personal question to answer, you will be introduced to the week's memory verse, and then you will write out a prayer in the space provided.

Days 2–4: Deep Dive into Scripture

These days are when we will dive deep into Scripture and start the interpretation process. You'll read the devotional thoughts and assigned Scripture passages, and you'll start to wrestle with the text and the questions. It's okay if you don't know the answers. Feel free to leave questions blank, as the goal isn't perfection; it's to know God more as we study the text and as He reveals Himself to us.

And just like Day 1, Days 2–4 will also have opportunities for memorizing verses.

Day 5: Reflection and Wrap-Up

This is the final day of each week's journey! Day 5 focuses more on application as you'll reflect on what you learned and look for ways to apply it to your everyday life. On this day you'll reread the passages again, work on your memory verse, and answer reflection and application questions.

You'll then write a prayer to God, which can be anything from praise to praying back Scripture to Him; or you can just journal your thoughts about the week's learning.

Memory Verse Work

In the appendix you'll find a resource with each of your weekly memory verse(s). Cut them out and use them however you'd like. Tape them to your mirror or hole punch them and put them on a ring to carry with you. They're included as an additional help to you throughout the study.

Pick Your Journey!

Listen, I get it. Some seasons do not allow for a deep dive into Scripture. I've had times when I wanted to do a Bible study, but I just didn't have a lot to give. You have three options for how to complete this study because even when life is hectic, being in the Word of God is important, as it is living and active, with the power to change and shape even the hardest (or most exhausted) hearts.

Journey A (2-day/week)**:** For those who are weary and just happy to show up, can I encourage you to do the following schedule? **Simply commit to doing Day 1 and Day 5 every week.** That's it. And if the memory verse is too much, write it out on those days but don't worry about memorizing it throughout the week.

Journey A is light on my words and heavy on Scripture. Days 1 and 5 don't have a lot of questions, but the ones they do have are repetitive so your brain will know what's coming after Week 1.

If you choose Journey A, I'm so glad you're here, and I cannot wait for God to use this journey to free you from striving.

Journey B (3-day/week)**:** This journey is for the woman who is ready to jump in, but is short on time. Instead of doing this as a 5-day study, make it a 3-day study. Here's what that would look like:

> **Day 1:** Complete Day 1's work as usual.
>
> **Day 2:** Instead of doing Days 2–4 as individual days, choose to complete the day that is focused on Colossians. There might be some references to previous days' work that you'll miss—but that's okay. Again, the goal isn't perfection but growth.
>
> **Day 3:** Complete Day 5's work as usual.

Journey C (5-day/week)**:** This study is designed to be a 5-day-a-week study with two rest days, but if you get behind, jump back up to Journey B for the week. The structure I've provided is a guide, but you have the freedom to take this journey however you and the Holy Spirit decide. Your worth isn't based on how well, how fast, or how thoroughly you complete this study. Your good God is excited to meet with you, but nothing can make Him adore you any more or any less. Enjoy the journey. I cannot wait to hear what God does through your faithfulness over the next six weeks.

What I love about this "pick your own journey" design is that you can do this study by yourself or with a group of women, and each woman can still participate in the group study but go at her own pace. But whatever journey you choose, I pray that you remember that no amount of time spent in Scripture is wasted:

> *As the rain and the snow come down from heaven, and to not return to it without watering the earth and making it bud and flourish, so that it yields seed for the sower and bread for the eater, so is my word that goes out from my mouth: It will not return to me empty, but will accomplish what I desire and achieve the purpose for which I sent it.*
>
> Isaiah 55:10–11

Colossians Quick Overview

Author: the apostle Paul while in prison in Rome

Type of Book: An Epistle or Letter

Date Written: Around AD 58–62

Audience: the church in Colossae

Big Ideas: the sufficiency of Christ, being rooted in Christ, standing firm against cultural pressures to add to the gospel

The Main Idea: Jesus is sufficient and the *only* one who can save us. Salvation doesn't come from worshiping many gods, like many in their culture practiced. And salvation doesn't come from observing Jewish laws and rituals. Salvation comes through Christ alone. Or as Patrick Schreiner states, the book is broken up into two ideas: 1) He [Christ] is sufficient, so 2) walk in Christ.[1]

Paul had actually never met the Colossians at the time this letter was written. But Epaphras, one of Paul's co-laborers in the faith, started the church and had shared with Paul about their growth, their love for one another, and also some of their struggles. And so, in the midst of suffering in prison, Paul took the time to write and encourage this body of believers and remind them of the truth of the gospel.

This short but powerful letter is a fantastic guide for the woman who wrestles with striving because it reminds us that Jesus is King over everything, and that devotion to Jesus frees us from cultural pressures and anything else that distracts from His great love for us.

The following page has a helpful and beautiful graphic from the book *The Visual Word* that illustrates the outline and big ideas of Colossians.

1. Patrick Schreiner and A. M. Benedetto, *The Visual Word: Illustrated Outlines of the New Testament Books* (Moody Publishers, 2021).

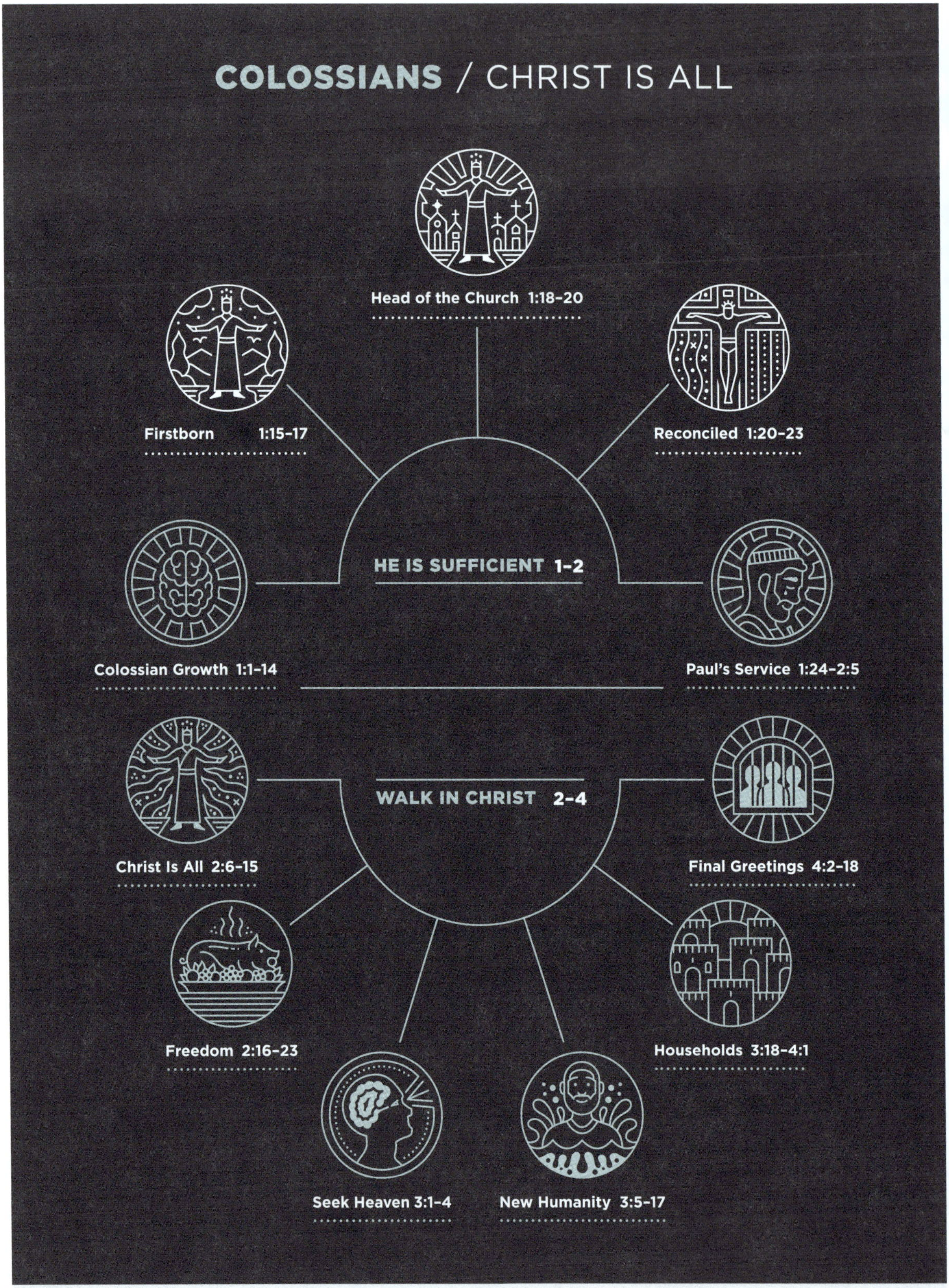

THE VISUAL WORD • **BY PATRICK SCHREINER** • DESIGNED BY ANTHONY BENEDETTO

WEEK ONE

RELATIONSHIP vs. RELIGION

Key passages for this week: Luke 10:38–42; Colossians 1:15–23, 2:6–15; Matthew 23

Introduction: Getting It Right

In the summer of 2025, Scottie Scheffler was considered the best golfer in the world. I am not a golfer. In fact, when I took golf lessons for my middle school PE credit, the instructor took one look at my swing and told me there was no hope for me and that this should be the last time I pick up a club. And it was. Other than the occasional putt-putt adventure (one during which I accidentally hit a first date in the head with my club; and no, we did not have a second date), I do not golf. But in 2025, I was captivated by a press conference in which Scottie was discussing his success. He ultimately came to this conclusion: "We work so hard for such little moments. . . . But at the end of the day, sometimes I just don't understand the point. . . . It feels like you work your whole life to celebrate winning a tournament for like a few minutes. It only lasts a few minutes."[2]

That resonated with me and evidently a lot of people because the video went viral. It's a common human experience to strive for something, get it, and then realize the satisfaction lasts only a moment, leaving you to strive after something else.

---

2 Nick Piastowski, "Scottie Scheffler's Actions Spoke Loudly in 2025. So Did His Words," *Golf News*, December 28, 2025, https://golf.com/news/scottie-schefflers-actions-2025-words/?amp=1&srsltid=AfmBOoqDm53t3zFE6MtME_SscSzS9n1rtapAoTjHIBsDXlgozRrJ3X_4.

Scottie's response prompted me to find out what all my golfing friends already knew: This guy is a believer! And when he won the Masters in 2024, he said something similar:

> I love winning. I hate losing. I really do. And when you're here in the biggest moments, when I'm sitting there with the lead on Sunday, I really, really want to win badly. And my buddies told me this morning, my victory was secure on the cross. And that's a pretty special feeling to know that I'm secure for forever and it doesn't matter if I win this tournament or lose this tournament. My identity is secure for forever.[3]

What Scottie is describing is what some theologians call Christian hedonism. The root of this idea is that our greatest joys and exhilarations are aligned with God's glorification. This idea can be summed up in one quote: "God is most glorified when we are most satisfied in him."[4]

> "God is most glorified when we are most satisfied in him."

This is the power of the cross! Our identities aren't wrapped up in being the best at our jobs; the best daughters, sisters, wives, or mothers; or in even being the best Christians possible. **The rat race is futile because Jesus paid it all.**

So why did I start this week, this whole Bible study with a story about golf (when I don't even like golf)?

As we begin, I want to get this one thing right. Each week we're looking at a choice that you get to make that will help you live free from striving and performance, and this week focuses on the most important choice of all: Will you choose relationship over religion?

A real relationship with Jesus, the God of the universe, is the only thing that satisfies our ultimate longings. No award, no mountaintop, no amount of working harder will produce anything except the need to keep chasing the next best thing.

---

3. Kevin Mercer, "Webb Simpson Podcast: PGA Tour Pro on Faith, Success & Golf," Sports Spectrum, March 26, 2026, https://sportsspectrum.com/podcast/2026/03/13/podcast-webb-simpson-golf-faith-success-augusta/.

4. John Piper, "God Is Most Glorified in Us When We Are Most Satisfied in Him," Desiring God, October 12, 2012, https://www.desiringgod.org/messages/god-is-most-glorified-in-us-when-we-are-most-satisfied-in-him.

A warning to those of us who have been in church or religious circles for quite some time: Just like the pharisees who prided themselves in following the Old Testament laws (as well as their hundreds of additional traditions and regulations), it's possible to transfer our efforts in worldly endeavors to religious ones. We can work so hard to do our Bible studies, go to church, and be seen as good and moral people that we can forget that our worth is rooted in a relationship with Jesus.

In fact, even with a study like this, if we don't get this first choice right, we can quickly shift from wanting to know Jesus better to simply wanting to complete another Bible study. Just look at the week titles. We can strive to have good character, to serve, to build community, to be grateful and generous, to be rooted—all good things—but we can do all those things and still miss the mark if we're doing them apart from Christ.

So, in this first week, I want to drive this home: **Apart from a relationship with Jesus as your Savior, nothing else matters**. All of it fades away. You can be the best of the best, know Scripture left and right, but if you don't have a relationship with the Author of love? Well, your faith is just empty religion, a clanging cymbal, noisy and pointless. And you will keep striving after the next thing in an attempt to satisfy your soul's greatest longing: Jesus.

Strivings cease at the feet of Jesus. They stop when you recognize that when God looks at you, He smiles and says, "That one's mine!" Strivings stop when you come to embrace your identity as a beloved child of a good, good Father. You will find ultimate freedom and satisfaction in Christ when you realize that you have access to an identity that you cannot earn.

And a person who is settled in *that* identity—well, that's a person who can freely choose relationship over religion, every time.

I want that for me. I want that for you. I want that for us.

So, when you're ready, turn the page, and let's continue this journey together.

Nothing to prove. Nothing to earn.

WEEK 1 | **DAY 1**

Big Picture Day

Today is our first Big Picture day! Remember that each Day 1 focuses on Scripture. You will simply read and allow the passages to "marinate" before sinking your teeth into the text. Here are three guidelines as you begin each reading:

- Read the Scripture passages for the week in one sitting.
- Highlight any verses, words, or themes that stick out to you.
- In the margins, write any questions you might have as you read.

Consider how the verses relate to each other and to the overall theme of the week.

Read Luke 10:38–42; Colossians 1:15–23, 2:6–15; Matthew 23

Now answer each of the questions below:

What does this passage(s) show me about God?

What does this passage show me about this world or humanity?

How does this passage apply to my life? Are there any principles that serve as a guide for the Christian life?

Memory Verse

Read this week's memory verse and write it below.

> *"Since, then, you have been raised with Christ, set your hearts on things above, where Christ is, seated at the right hand of God."* COLOSSIANS 3:1

Prayer

Ephesians 2:8-9 says, "For it is by grace you have been saved, through faith—and this is not from yourselves, it is the gift of God—not by works, so that no one can boast."

Pray through the passage in your own words. If you're not sure how to do this, feel free to use or tweak the example prayer below.

Lord, Your Word tells me that I am saved through Your grace alone, that there's nothing I can do to earn my salvation, but it's a gift from You. Father, thank You for the gift of salvation through faith, but more than that, thank You that because of Christ, I don't have to earn my good standing with You. Help me to believe this deep in my bones so that I'm not tempted to try to earn my salvation or prove my worth. When my heart starts to wander toward works-based thinking, guide my heart back to resting in Your work alone. When my heart starts to meander toward self-righteousness, guide my heart back to only boasting in You and You alone. God, if there are any areas of my life where I'm striving to earn Your favor, Lord, would You bring those areas to mind now? I confess and entrust them to You. Help me to set my heart on things above this week. In Jesus' holy name, Amen.

Who Am I Becoming?

Luke 10:38–42

In the gospel of Luke, we're introduced to two sisters, Martha and Mary. Martha opened her home to Jesus and the disciples, and she was busy with all the many preparations needed to host guests. Can you imagine hosting your Lord and Savior, and the care and effort you would put into getting your home ready and serving your guests? Mary, on the other hand, sat at Jesus' feet rather than helping her sister.

This would be a recipe for disaster in any family—or at least it would be in mine! It is not an uncommon occurrence for my kids to squabble about whose turn it is to unload the dishwasher or take out the trash. So, as one can imagine, some sisterly drama ensued.

Read Luke 10:38–39 and answer the questions below.

Look at verse 38. Do you notice anything peculiar about who welcomed Jesus?

In that time period, it would have been highly unorthodox for a Jewish leader to be welcomed by a woman. This is a powerful moment and one that we might overlook for two reasons: 1) it's not the big idea of the passage, and 2) it is very common in our faith communities for women to serve in the ways that Martha did. But during this time period, it just wasn't so. Jesus was more concerned about welcoming the kingdom of heaven and its ways here on earth than following cultural norms. From the beginning, the mission of Jesus was to love and to save and welcome both men and women into His kingdom and invite them to live on mission for Him.

Sister, your life, your ministry, is important in the kingdom of God. **Jesus absolutely welcomes you and wants a relationship with *you*.**

Luke 10:38 begins, "As Jesus and his disciples were on their way . . ." Martha wasn't just welcoming a few people into her home, she had a whole crew!

Have you ever experienced the stress of preparing your home for a group of people? If so, what is your typical response?

Look at vs. 39. What are some of the differences you've observed between Mary and Martha in this passage?

At this point in the story, out of the two sisters, which one do you most identify with and why?

Read Luke 10:40–42 and answer the questions below.

Verse 40 states that Martha was ________________________ by all the work that she had to do. What was her work keeping her from?

Martha approached Jesus and basically said, "Lord, I'm going to need You to set my sister straight and tell her to help me out!" But Jesus' response wasn't what Martha expected. Reread Luke 10:41–42 and write down Jesus' words to Martha below:

If you were told that your sibling's or other loved one's response or choice was "better" than yours, how would you respond?

When I was a child, I thought Jesus was simply warning Martha about being too busy. This was the main point I took away: *Don't get so busy that you miss the important things in life.* And yes, that is one lesson. But as I've studied the passage, I no longer believe that the main message is about being busy vs. being present.

It's about who Martha and Mary were becoming.

Martha was becoming a frustrated and worn-out woman from all of her "doing" for Jesus. Mary, on the other hand, was becoming a person who sat at His feet, adored Him, and listened to Him. Jesus was not inviting Martha away from her tasks; He was inviting her to become a person who was more enamored with God Himself. **He wanted her to become a person who longed to sit in the presence of God more than she longed to do things *for* Him.**

Think about that for a minute and then look at the concepts below.

What does "doing" for Jesus look like in this passage? In the first two categories, list 1 to 3 things you notice in the story of Martha and Mary. Then, in the next two, list 1 to 3 ways you are "doing" and "being" in your own life.

What does it look like when you're busy doing things for Jesus and when you're living from a place of being enamored with Jesus?

Doing for Jesus (in the passage):	Being enamored with Jesus (in the passage):
Doing for Jesus (in my life):	Being enamored with Jesus (in my life):

I don't know what you put in your columns, but one thing I wrote down was this: When I'm trying to do the most for Jesus, I end up exhausted, burnt out, and although I hate to admit it, a little bitter.

But the passage we've read today offers us a better way forward. It's a story about having a relationship with God, rather than being worn out by doing things for God.

One pastor said it this way:

> True religion is when you serve God to get nothing else but more of God. Many people use religion as a way of getting something else from God they want—blessings, rewards, even escape from judgment. This is wearisome to us, and to God. But when God is His own reward, Christianity becomes thrilling. Sacrifice becomes joy.[5]

Do you see where we're going? Just like this passage of Scripture is about who Mary and Martha were becoming, this is a study about who *you're* becoming.

Relationship with a good and faithful God looks like loving and serving God without expecting anything in return other than His love; it's about who we are becoming in Christ! Religion, on the other hand, is the idea that our acceptance and place in the kingdom are earned through how much we do for Jesus. The first concept leads to freedom from striving and performance, but the latter leads to a weary life of proving oneself over and over again.

Over the next five weeks, you'll be given opportunities to make choices about the person you're becoming. And all of that is good and healthy; but if those choices aren't rooted in the understanding that the God of the universe wants a relationship with you, you'll end up like Martha, tired and worn out from doing good things for Jesus. What God wants from us is to be like Mary, sitting at His feet, desiring a relationship with Him more than anything else.

Sometimes I'm more comfortable chasing down and doing good things for Jesus rather than just being with Him. If you are like me and you're a doer, let me give you a tip: Every time the urge to add something to your to-do list kicks in, stop and reframe that decision into a question—not "What can I do?" or "How do I do this better?" Instead, **"Who am I becoming?"**

- "Am I becoming a person who is chasing stages, or am I becoming a person who chases opportunities to serve others?"
- "Am I becoming a person who is chasing perfection, or am I a person who is choosing proximity instead?"

---

5. This is JD Greear summarizing Tim Keller on religion vs. relationship in JD Greear, *Gospel: Recovering the Power that Made Christianity Revolutionary* (B&H Publishing Group, 2011), 32–33.

- "Am I a person who is trying to do the most for Jesus, or am I a person who is so enamored with Him that I can't help but want to be with Him?"

Can you see the difference?

Sure, you'll have to make adjustments, but as you intentionally choose to focus on your relationship with God, you will inevitably become more like Christ, which will lead you to a more satisfied life.

Memory Verse

Read Colossians 3:1 and then try your best to fill in the blanks from memory below (but remember, it's okay if you need to look back at Scripture!).

"Since, ____________, you have been ________________ with ________________, set your ________________ on ________________ ________________, where ________________ is, ________________ at the ________________ hand of ________."

Prayer

Feel free to pray this prayer or write out your own prayer to God below.

God, thank You for being a God who offers us rest in You. Thank You for sending Jesus so that I can have a real, genuine relationship with You instead of having to earn my salvation. Lord, help me to become a person who longs to sit in Your holy presence more than I long to do things for You. Change my heart to long for Your presence more than anything else this world has to offer. In Jesus' name, Amen.

KEY TAKEAWAY: Because of the good news of Jesus, we get to become women who long to be in the presence of God more than we long to do things for Him.

In Christ: Nothing to Prove, Nothing to Earn

Colossians 1:15–23; 2:1–15

I recently grabbed coffee with a neighbor who describes herself as "religious but not churchy." When I asked her what that meant, she said, "I believe in a God and I try to do more good than harm, but I don't really feel like I fit in with church folks." Her understanding of religion was trying to do more good than bad in order to earn God's approval and a spot in heaven.

This is a fairly common understanding of religion. Religion is a combination of beliefs and practices that help people express their understanding of both a higher power and their purpose for existence. Many religions use rituals, moral codes, and behavior modification to help their followers earn good standing with their god(s). So, it's not surprising that many of our neighbors, friends, and even family members hold to the belief that being a "good" Christian simply means doing more good than harm in order to earn the approval of God.

And before we get too judgy of this religious view, let's be honest. Sometimes, we too live as though the more we do for God, the more He loves us or approves of us. But this does not align with Scripture.

While the world tells us to do better, be a good person, and earn our right standing with God, the Bible tells us that in Christ and Christ alone we are offered life and life abundantly.[6] And just like we haven't earned our salvation, we don't earn God's love, generosity, mercy, and favor!

---

6. John 10:10.

This is the difference between religion and relationship. Religion says do more, be better. A relationship with Jesus tells us, "Come to me, all you who are weary and burdened, and I will give you rest."[7]

This is the key to truly living like we have nothing to prove and nothing to earn, and not just swapping one set of striving behaviors for another.

And if the purpose of this first week is to rightly understand that in Christ, because of His saving work on the cross, we have nothing to prove and nothing to earn, we need to know exactly how that can be true! Who is this Jesus who has made a way for us to choose relationship over religion?

I can think of no better epistle to study than Colossians!

This short but mighty epistle packs a punch as it answers the questions "Who is the Christ?" and "How do we now live, knowing who Christ is?" And so, as we read the passages today, we're going to take a thorough look at the person in whom we are rooting our identity: Jesus.

Read Colossians 1:15–20 and answer the questions below.

While you're reading this passage, underline or highlight every instance of the phrase "in Him/Christ" or "with Him/Christ." How many times do you see this phrase?

In the space below, list all of the ways that Jesus is described in this passage.

7. Matthew 11:28.

Read Colossians 1:21–25 and answer the questions below.

Verses 15–20 discuss who Jesus is, but verses 21–25 talk about what He's done for us.

How does verse 21 describe our spiritual state?

We were ____________________ from God and were ____________________ in our minds because of our ____________ ____________________.

What two words come right after this passage, starting in verse 22? Write them down below. Underline them. Highlight them. Celebrate them!

Think about those small but powerful words for a moment. We were alienated from God's goodness and grace; we were separated and unable to make our way to Him. No matter how much we strive or how hard we try to be and do good, we are unable to bridge the gap that only the Savior of the world could bridge.

But now . . .

But now He has reconciled you by Christ's physical body, His death, burial, and resurrection. Jesus conquered death so that you and I could be ________________ to Him and he can now present us as ____________________________, without ________________ and free from ________________. (v. 22)

Let's look at the contrasts between verses 21 to 22.

Verse 21	*Verse 22*
You were ____________________	*But now* ____________________
You were ____________________	*But now* ____________________
Because of ____________________	*But now because of* ____________________
	____________________
	You are free from ____________________

I need you to know that as I write this, I'm in a coffee shop trying my best not to have a praise break. Because "but now" is good news!

Your darkest moments can never keep you from the love of God, and your best and brightest moments can't earn your favor with Him either. This is the good news of Jesus.

This is the gospel.[8]

In Jesus, your strivings can cease because in Christ you have nothing to prove and everything to gain. Tim Keller says it this way,

> It is one thing to understand the gospel but is quite another to experience the gospel in such a way that it fundamentally changes us and becomes the source of our identity and security.[9]

Read Colossians 2:1–7.

Since we've received Christ as our Lord, how are we supposed to live our lives? What are the three descriptions of lives rooted in Jesus?

1.

2.

3.

Do you notice that two of these three things have qualifiers? You're not just supposed to be rooted and built up. You're rooted and built up_____ _________(hint: verse 7)!

---

8. JD Greear, *Gospel: Recovering the Power that Made Christianity Revolutionary* (B&H Publishing Group, 2011), 67.

9. Ibid., xv.

You are not miraculously strengthened in the faith all by yourself; you're strengthened _____ ________ ____________ as you were taught (hint: second part of verse 7)!

And lastly, this one is on you. You are overflowing with gratitude, which is a choice that only you can make.

Scripture tells us that we can be grateful in *all things* and every season, which tells us that this isn't a personality trait, but an act of obedience, a choice, a discipline that we practice.

Out of those three descriptors of how we should live our lives, which do you find the easiest and the hardest? Why?

Relationship with a good and faithful God looks like a life rooted in *Him*, connected to His people, and grateful in every season! Religion, on the other hand, is the idea that the more we do for God the more He loves us or approves of us. *Which one sounds more freeing and more fulfilling to you?*

Read Colossians 2:8–15 and answer the questions below.

In his letter to the Colossians, Paul warns believers not to be deceived by false teaching that might lead them astray from the truest message. One commentary says it this way, "Those trying to lead the Colossians astray were not 'bad people' in respect to conventional morals. They may even have exceeded many of the Christians in their lifestyle. Moreover, they were sincere. Their sophisticated language, their stringent rationality within the system, and their self-conscious morality made a huge, religious Venus flytrap."[10]

10. R. Kent Hughes, *Philippians, Colossians, and Philemon: The Fellowship of the Gospel and the Supremacy of Christ* (Crossway, 2013), 274.

In other words, the Colossians were being warned about being tempted to choose a hollow religion instead of relationship with the one true God. And they weren't being lured away by overtly bad ideologies! Some of their messages or even the messengers had the appearance of some good in them.

In my own life, one of the more "hollow philosophies" I have had to fight against is that if I live a moral life for Jesus, I'm entitled to a good life full of "blessings" or in other words, "more." And I think this is a common experience for many of us.

Many in our society are chasing "more:" a bigger house, a better car, more vacations, more extracurriculars for their kids, health and wellness, more, more, more. On the outside, this life full of "blessings" can seem like the ultimate goal, but the way of Jesus is an upside-down kingdom where we find our fulfillment in Him instead of worldly endeavors. *Moody Commentary* said this of the Colossians facing these false teachings, "They need no other sources of spiritual wealth, since the fullness of Deity dwells in Him [Christ]."[11]

In your life, can you identify any hollow and deceptive philosophies that can distract you from your relationship with God?

When or where are you most exposed to "hollow and deceptive" philosophies? How do you combat these messages?

11. "Colossians," by Gerald Peterman, *The Moody Bible Commentary*, gen. eds. Michael Rydelnik and Michael Vanlaningham (Moody, 2014), 1867.

Let's look at what Paul says. In verse 8, he warns the Colossians about these deceptive messages, but then his next sentences (verses 9–15) are devoted to talking about . . . what?

Do you see the contrast? Rather than dismantling the arguments of the hollow philosophies, he points to a truer and greater message. He is reminding the readers of his letter that, because of Christ, they have nothing to prove, nothing to earn! Because of Christ, they are invited to choose a relationship with the almighty God instead of the bondage of religion.

Spend some time rereading verses 9–15, and in your own words, write out the descriptions of Christ and what He's done for you.

In light of what you've read today, is there one thing the Holy Spirit is prompting you to reflect on? What change might you make in your life so that you can choose relationship with an almighty God instead of the emptiness of religion?

Memory Verse

Read Colossians 3:1 and then try to fill in the blanks from memory below.

"Since, ____,
set your ____, where
Christ is, ______________________________________." Colossians 3:1

Prayer

Feel free to pray this prayer or write out your own prayer to God below.

God, thank You for coming to earth and becoming human. Thank You for Christ and His precious life, His sacred death, and His life-changing resurrection. God, give me eyes to see Your truth as greater than the empty lies this world has to offer. God, keep my heart from leaning toward false religion or simply behavior modification, and keep my eyes fixed on You. You paid it all, just so I could have a relationship with You. Lord, let it be so. Guide my steps and heart in such a way for this to be true of my life. Amen.

KEY TAKEAWAY: Christ has paid it all! He's done it all! So, by choosing a relationship with Him, you can choose to have nothing to prove and nothing to earn.

Choosing Relationship

Matthew 23

Today we're examining a tough piece of Scripture. I have a distinct memory of hearing a sermon on Matthew 23 as a young adult, and I walked away fearful, wondering if I was a Pharisee. I was in seminary. I loved Jesus. But I was striving to earn right standing with God. And so, I left that sermon shaking and afraid and full of shame (instead of conviction), which leads me to saying this on the front end: **Shame is not the goal of today's study.**

Although this passage is a warning, and I want us to wrestle with these warnings, there is a distinction between shame and conviction that I want to explain.

Shame is fear-based and keeps the focus on you. It says, "You've messed up. You are getting it wrong and you'll never get it right. How dare you? You should have known better!"

C. S. Lewis says it this way, "I sometimes think that shame, mere awkward, senseless shame, does as much towards preventing good acts and straightforward happiness as any of our vices can do."[12]

And I absolutely agree with him. Shame and blame are tools that Satan uses to keep you knocked down, defeated, and focused on the wrong thing. And you can identify the voice of shame because although shame can rightly identify a problem, its condemnation is fixated on you—instead of the sin—as it screams, "You! You! *You* are the problem!"

In contrast, conviction is the work of the Holy Spirit, and it says, "You've messed up, but Jesus has already paid the price for that and is inviting you into a different way

12. C.S. Lewis, *A Grief Observed* (Faber & Faber, 1961), 41

of living. Come and live." Conviction starts with your failure (or the world's general brokenness), but it doesn't leave you there. It fixes your gaze on the One who has paid the price for your sin. Do you see the difference?

Shame produces fear. It keeps us navel-gazing. It keeps us focused on ourselves. And often only leads to short-term changes. And then when we fail the cycle of shame starts again.

Conviction produces hope and is a catalyst for true and lasting change. It keeps our eyes fixed on Jesus and His great love for us, and His invitation to living a better, truer, more hope-filled life.

In some religious circles, we've used shame to manipulate people into doing right rather than allowing the work of the Holy Spirit to convict and shepherd people into a new way of living. This is a form of behavior modification. Actions are changed (often temporarily), but the heart is neglected.

I don't want our reading to do that today.

Instead, allow Scripture to speak to you; but if you start feeling shame, remind yourself of the question that we've been asking this week. The question is not what can I do or change for Jesus; it's **who am I becoming?**

Read Matthew 23:1–12.

Who was Jesus speaking to?

This is important because if He is speaking to believers or potential believers, He's highlighting the way to true life! ***What do you think it means when Jesus says, "You must be careful to do everything they tell you. But do not do what they do" (v. 3)?***

Verses 3–7 offers a rather scathing description of Pharisees. List out how they're described below.

Take an honest moment for reflection. Does any of that ring true for parts of your own life? If so, jot down areas or potential areas that might be in need of some conviction (no shaming allowed!).

I'll be honest—some of these descriptions of the Pharisees ring true for me! I've been at conferences or Christian events and have longed to be at certain tables or rooms, and I've longed to be treated with respect in my own marketplace (the field of teaching). Remember, the goal isn't to have *never* experienced those things. We're all human, and temptation to sin is part of the human experience. But the question is, has the Spirit ever convicted you when those longings have produced a life in which your actions model verse 5: "Everything they do is done for people to see"?

Look at verses 8–12, what is the main idea of this passage? (Hint: it's summarized in verses 11–12)

Read Matthew 23:13–39.

In this section of Scripture, who is Jesus speaking to directly?

This is important because in the previous section Jesus was talking *about* the Pharisees, albeit in front of them, to the disciples and crowd. But at this point in His sermon, He shifts comments from being about them to speaking directly *to* them.

In this passage Jesus says, "Woe to you!" how many times?

The book of Matthew lists seven woes. In the first column of the chart below, name/title each woe in your own words. In the second column, describe what Scripture has to say about each.

Woes	Description of Woes
Example: **Woe #1** Kingdom Blockers	Rather than being people who lead the way to the kingdom of God, they do the opposite and shut the door, blocking others from the kingdom.
Woe #2	
Woe #3	
Woe #4	

Woe #5	
Woe #6	
Woe #7	

What do you notice about these woes? Do you notice any similar themes? Who are the Pharisees helping or hurting?[13]

Do any of these woes spark conviction in your own life? In what way?

---

13. Fun fact: In some translations of the Bible, there are eight woes, but newer translations leave out the eighth as there is debate on whether verse 14 (where the missing woe is listed) was originally included in chapter 23. Most agree that although Scripture is clear about the sins listed in this "missing woe," verse 14 was probably not included in the original writing of Matthew and added later. However, if you're the curious type, explore Mark 12:40 and Luke 20:47 to see what this extra woe would warn against.

Read Matthew 23:37–39.

Look at the end of verse 37. What is the heart of Jesus in this? What was His hope and goal of all of this?

In light of the passage today and the saving power of Jesus we talked about yesterday, I want you to wrestle with our main question again: **"Who am I becoming?"**

Take a few minutes to think about the last few months or maybe even years and ask the question: Who have I become? And then think about your present and future and wrestle with the question: Who am I becoming?

Use the word cloud to choose words to answer both questions, or feel free to write in other words that might come to mind.

Anxious Generous Bitter Patient Wise Stressed

Grateful Grumpy Joyful Argumentative Content Kind

Jealous Peaceful Angry Stuck Grudge-holder

Who have I become?	Who am I becoming?

Memory Verse

Write Colossians 3:1 below, and then speak the words aloud three times, working from memory as best you can. Feel free to use your Bible as needed.

Prayer

Is there anything on your heart that stands out from today's lesson? Spend some time talking to the Lord about it. Write out your prayer below.

KEY TAKEAWAY: In Christ, I have nothing to prove and nothing to earn, so I can freely choose relationship over religion because the God of the universe has invited me to be His beloved child.

WEEK 1 | **DAY 5**

Reflection and Wrap-Up

Over the last four days we've learned:

- Christ has paid it all! He's done it all! In Him, you have nothing to prove and nothing to earn.
- When it comes to doing the most for Jesus, He cares more about who we are becoming.
- In our search for significance, we can also mistake religion for a relationship with Him. Jesus invites us to choose relationship over religion, every time.

Today is a shorter day. Reread one or all of the passages we read this week and spend some time journaling below by using the provided prompts.

Passages from the week:
Luke 10:38–42; Colossians 1:15–23, 2:6–15; Matthew 23.

What is one theme or truth from Scripture that stood out to you the most this week?

Has anything from this week changed, challenged, or shaped your thinking, your actions, or beliefs? If so, how?

What is one idea or verse that has encouraged you that you'd like to carry with you?

In light of what you've learned this week, a relationship with Jesus . . .

Finish the sentence: Because of Christ, I . . .

Memory Verse

Write Colossians 3:1 from memory, below. If you can't, no worries! Grace upon grace! Write it out using your Bible as a reference.

Prayer

Spend some time talking to God below. Take what you just reflected on and turn it into a prayer. Thank God for what He's shown you this week and ask Him to help you carry it forward.

KEY TAKEAWAY: Because of Christ, I have nothing to prove, nothing to earn. He's paid it all! And in light of this truth, I can choose relationship over religion and live *freely in Him* as a beloved child of God.

WEEK TWO

CHARACTER vs. CHARISMA

Key passages for this week: Colossians 3; Matthew 7:13–29; 1 Samuel 16

Introduction: God Sees the Heart

Have you ever been at an event, maybe an office party or a friend's birthday party, and everyone is like, "Oh my word, you have to meet so and so; they are so fun and just the life of the party!" And while the rest of your friends swoon at their charisma and jokes, there is something inside of you that doesn't feel right. Your intuition suspects their charisma only goes skin deep, and what's underneath lacks true character. Or maybe you've seen this firsthand. What once seemed shiny and flashy was rather dull on the inside after the person's true character was revealed.

I love that we serve a God who tells us that He cares more about what's on the inside than on the outside (1 Sam. 16:7). In fact, **God has a habit of regularly picking underdogs, outsiders, and misfits—people the world completely disregards—and He chooses to work through them for His glory.**

Scripture tells us that King David was a man after God's own heart, and yet we see in 1 Samuel 16 that he was the runt of his brothers. When God sent Samuel to find a replacement for King Saul, David's father, Jesse, did not even present him as an option for kingship. Jesse was so certain that his stronger, older, and more strapping sons would be chosen that he left David behind to care for the sheep.

Can you imagine?! Your own father is so unimpressed with your stature and ability that he sends you off to shepherd the sheep. Even Samuel, when he first laid eyes on David's brother Eliab, was certain he must be the Lord's anointed. But God told Samuel:

"Do not consider his appearance or his height, for I have rejected him. The Lord does not look at the things people look at. People look at the outward appearance, but the Lord looks at the heart."[14]

In a world that values success, quick results, and flashy things, character is in short supply. And yet God is all about it. He is after the good stuff: our truest hearts. This is also why last week we learned about having a real relationship with Jesus instead of choosing the pretense of religion. And it's why this week, one of the keys to learning how to stop striving is to mirror our good Father and to choose to focus on our character instead of the shallowness of charisma.

Although charisma in and of itself isn't bad, when it's empty or only goes skin-deep, it comes up lacking every time. **Charisma, without good character, keeps us chasing others' approval, while character keeps us deeply rooted to what God says matters most: loving Him and loving others**. Charisma can keep us focused on ourselves and how we appear and are perceived, while character keeps us connected to our values and our identity in Christ. One can keep us fixated on ourselves in an unhealthy way, and the other helps us understand who we are and whose we are and how we should then live. One can lead us to a life much like the Pharisees', and the other leads to a life of freedom found in a relationship with Jesus.

14. 1 Samuel 16:7.

Big Picture Day

Thus far in the study we've learned that as believers who are learning to stop striving, we must choose . . .

Relationship instead of religion (Week 1)

And this week we'll be learning to choose character instead of charisma (Week 2).

Big Picture Questions

Today is our Big Picture day! Remember that each Day 1 focuses on Scripture. You will simply read and allow the passages to "marinate" before sinking your teeth into the text. Here are three guidelines as you begin each reading:

- Read the Scripture passages for the week in one sitting.
- Highlight any verses, words, or themes that stick out to you.
- In the margins, write any questions you might have as you read.

Consider how the verses relate to each other and to the overall theme of the week.

Read Colossians 3; Matthew 7:13–29; 1 Samuel 16.

Now answer each of the questions below:

What does this passage(s) show me about God?

What does this passage show me about this world or humanity?

How does this passage apply to my life? Are there any principles that serve as a guide for the Christian life?

Prayer

Read 1 Samuel 16:7 and Psalm 139:23–24. We could quickly make this week's focus "Be Better. Do this good thing. Choose Character vs. Charisma." But in light of what we learned last week, reflect on your choice to pursue relationship vs. religion. Ask your good Father, who looks more on the heart than outward appearances, to search your heart and go before you this week. Ask Him to lead you this week to again answer the question, "Who am I becoming? Am I a person who cares more about developing true godly character? Or am I a person who tends to care more about the appearance of character instead of the true thing itself?" Spend some time talking to God about this (write out your prayer below).

Memory Verse

Refresh your memorization of Colossians 3:1, and then read this week's memory verse, Colossians 3:2, and write it below.

"Set your minds on things above, not on earthly things." COLOSSIANS 3:2

Holy and Deeply Loved

Colossians 3:1–17

I'm not sure about you, but I like the idea of growing in character. In reality, I'm better at appearing to have it. I love the idea of being deeply rooted in my identity in Christ so much that I don't worry what my friends or neighbors think about me; however, I'm more susceptible to wanting their approval than I'd like to admit.

Just this morning I opened my phone and started to scroll. I quickly felt the urge to post something—anything—that would garner likes and comments. There are a thousand different ways we all wrestle with this, but today's passage isn't here to shame us for our wrestling. It serves as a road map to answer the questions: How do we change? How do we become women of character, transformed by a God who can redeem any heart?

Let's look and see.

Read Colossians 3:1–4 and answer the questions below.

Look at the very first sentence. Who is the author, Paul, talking to in this passage? How exactly does he describe this specific audience?

This is important! Paul is not saying that all people should behave a certain way, but only people who have been raised ”with Christ”—in other words, those who are true believers! It also means—and this is equally important—that we truly cannot do this on our own. It's not natural to want to choose relationship over religion and character over charisma. Dying to ourselves and becoming a new person isn't possible in our own flesh; but because we have been raised to life with Christ, we can live lives free with nothing to prove and nothing to earn!

Do you notice any repeated language in verses 1–4? What command is stated twice in these verses?

In the NIV, this passage tells us to set our hearts on things above and to set our minds on things above (vv. 1–2). Translations like the New King James Version word the verses this way: "Seek those things which are above . . . Set your mind on things above." I love the NIV's translation that uses the imagery of both our heart's *and* mind's involvement in seeking things above!

What does it look like to seek the things that are above with both your heart and your mind?

What are we explicitly told not to set our minds on? Do you find that easy or difficult?

Read Romans 12:1–2 and 2 Corinthians 5:16–21. What similarities do you see in these passages? What additional encouragement did you find?

Look at Colossians 3:3–4. Why do we set our hearts and minds on things above?

The first few verses of this chapter remind us that we are raised with Christ (v. 1), our lives are hidden with Christ (v. 2), and we will one day be revealed with Christ in glory! So, no matter what we face on this earth, we are called to live out of that reality. And that reality changes everything—especially in the battle between character vs. charisma.

When our hearts and minds are set on things above, the development of our character will follow suit. But when our hearts and minds are set on the things of this world, we focus more on maintaining the appearance of good or keeping up with the Joneses (or whatever type of striving that our individual hearts are bent toward). **In the battle of character vs. charisma, character wins every time. It is what will lead us to a life free of striving and performance.**

Read Colossians 3:5–17 and answer the questions below.

Summarize verse 5 below.

Notice that the list of things to "put to death" is not all-encompassing, as Paul prefaces the list with "Whatever belongs to your earthly nature." You might look at that initial list and think that you don't wrestle with any of those things, but do you have a "Whatever" that belongs to your earthly nature that you'd like to identify and put to death?

If so, write it below.

Verses 8 and 9 provide another list of things we are told to either put to death or get rid of. I've compiled both lists below.

In the space beside each item, write a modern-day, culturally "acceptable" way for someone to participate in these sins that needs to be put to death. Feel free to look up the definitions of these words for extra credit or if you need to know what they mean.

Sexual immorality	E.g., Scrolling and looking at things on my phone (could be pornography or could just be considered inappropriate) that cause me to lust. Reading fiction that causes my heart to sin.
Immorality	
Impurity	
Lust	
Evil desires	
Greed/Idolatry	

Anger	
Rage	
Malice	
Slander	
Filthy Language	
Lying	

Colossians 3:7 reminds us that these behaviors are things we used to do *before* we followed Christ! All of us! You. Me. All believers. We all have sinned and fallen short of the glory of God (Rom. 3:23).

But now that we're living in Christ, we're called to a better way of living where our character matters. Charisma might take this list and work on the most culturally offensive ones while still secretly nursing some of the more culturally accepted ones. But as Colossians 3:1–4 reminds us, because we are raised with Christ, hidden with Christ, and will one day be with Him in glory, we are called to care about our character and kill any sin that is slowly eating away at it.

Summarize Colossians 3:11 below.

Why do you think Paul added verse 11?

In your Bible, circle "therefore" in verse 12. Write "because of this" with an arrow pointing to the previous verses.

Read the "becauses" below and then fill in the missing words from verse 12.

- Because we are raised with Christ, hidden with Christ, and will one day appear with Him in glory (vv. 1–4) . . .
- Because we are putting to death the sinful ways that chip away at our character (vv. 5–9) . . .
- Because we are putting on a new self that is being renewed in Christ (v. 10) . . .
- Because we are united in Christ (v. 11) . . .

"Therefore, as God's chosen people __________ and ______________ ______________."

What are we now called to do?

Circle the words "holy" and "dearly loved" in verse 12. Above it write "I am," and then draw an arrow to those two words.

Sister, I want to pause right here for just a moment and encourage you with this good news. Because of Christ, when God looks at you, He sees you as His holy and dearly loved child.

I have six children, and at the writing of this study I have a chunky little baby boy. I regularly have to stop writing and tend to him. In fact, many of this week's lessons were written while I rocked or held him. This is no burden, as I delight in my son. I see his presence in my life as a miracle, a true gift. He is absolutely beloved. As I'm typing this, I paused to look at his sleeping face and kiss his baby cheeks. My love for him is fierce and knows no bounds. And yet, the intense love of a mother for her newborn only gives us a mere glimpse of God's perfect love for us.

You are His beloved daughter. He has called you out of bondage to sin and has given you a new life in Christ. This is your identity, and it is greater than any identity this world has to offer. And because of this good news, you don't have to strive to be somebody you're not because you're already His. You belong to Him, and you get to live a life free from striving and performance because of that belovedness (not a word, but I'm making it up, and we'll see if my editors keep it).

Below, I want you to write the words "In Christ, I am holy and dearly loved." And I want you to never forget it. Write it on a sticky note; hang it on your bathroom mirror or wherever you look at yourself. But let these words sink down into your heart until they ring true.

According to Colossians 3:12–14, what does good character look like for someone who is holy and dearly loved?

Which one of these virtues provides an opportunity for you to grow in your character?

Do verses 12–14 remind you of any other passages in the New Testament? If so, reference them below. If not, that's okay! We'll be going over a similar passage on Day 4.

Now reread verses 15–17, and then look back at verses 1–4. Do you notice any similarities?

In the beginning of chapter 3, we're told to set our hearts and minds on things above. In verses 15–17, we're again told to use our hearts and minds.

How are we supposed to set our hearts on things above? Fill in the blanks below.

"Let the peace of Christ rule in your ________________, since you are members of ________ ____________ you were called to peace. And be ________________." (Colossians 3:15)

How are we supposed to set our minds on things above?

"Let the message of Christ ________________ among you __________________ as you teach and admonish one another with all ________________ through psalms, hymns, and songs from the __________, singing to God with __________________ in your hearts." (Colossians 3:16)

And how do we put these beliefs into practice and allow them to transform our lives (and character)?

"And ________________________ you do, whether in word or ______________, do it _____ in the name of the Lord Jesus, giving ________________ to God the Father through him." (Colossians 3:17)

If we want to choose to have character over charisma, our hearts and minds must be set on things above to the point that it changes the things we do (vv. 12–14) and the things we don't do (vv. 5–11). **When our hearts and minds are set on Christ, it changes how we live our lives.** It frees us from the pressures of chasing fame, others' approval, success in our work, etc., and it focuses our hearts on what matters most: being called holy and deeply loved by a good God. This reality changes everything, and it shapes us into women of godly character who aren't consumed with our own (or others') charisma.

Memory Verse

Refresh your memorization of Colossians 3:2 and then write the memory verse for this week below.

"Set your ________________________ on things ________________________, not on ________________________ things." (Colossians 3:2)

Prayer

You can pray this prayer or write out one below.

Lord, would You set our hearts and minds on You? God, take away every distraction, and help me live a life free from the pressure of chasing the approval of others. God, would You remind me this week, that I am Yours and that I was made to be holy and deeply loved by You? Let this be my anthem this week. In Jesus' holy name, amen.

KEY TAKEAWAY: When our hearts and minds are set on Christ, it changes how we live. It frees us from the pressures of things like chasing fame, others' approval, success in our work, and it focuses our hearts on what matters most: being called holy and deeply loved by a good God.

WEEK 2 | **DAY 3**

The Narrow Way and the Wide Way

Matthew 7:13–29

Yesterday, we discussed that choosing character over charisma requires us to set our hearts and minds on Christ. Today, we're going to look at three comparisons found in Scripture that show us the difference between a charismatic life and a life of true character.

Read Matthew 7:13–14 and answer the questions below.

Based only on this brief reading, what do you think this passage is about?

When I was growing up, I assumed this passage was *only* talking about the path to heaven and to hell. I had only heard it preached referring to our eternal journeys, not our present-day ones. But take a look at this passage again. I want us to lay our presuppositions aside and look at what it states:

"Enter through the narrow gate. For wide is the gate and broad is the road that leads to ________________________, and many enter through it. But small is the gate and narrow the road that leads to __________, and only a few find it." (Matthew 7:13–14)

Notice those blanks don't say hell and heaven. ***What do they say? Underline those words and then jump with me over to John 10.***

Turn to John 10:1–10 and read the passage. Who is Jesus talking to?

Who does Jesus identify as the gate?

Jesus says, "I am the gate; whoever enters through me will be ______________" (v. 9).

Where does this gate lead to (v. 10)?

Jesus says that He, the gatekeeper, has come so that His sheep might have life and life to the *full*. And although, yes, this passage in John is referring to our life to come and our salvation, notice the passage is referring to present tense life, the here and now, as well! This is important to understand: Salvation in Christ isn't just for eternal security. For those who are in Christ, we are new creations. We are saved here and now and in the life to come. This changes the way we live our days!

Looking back at our passage today, one theologian broke down this passage in Matthew by saying that walking through the narrow gate is our salvation, our "evangelical decision" (the moment we trust Jesus); but then continuing to walk this narrow path is our "ethical endurance."[15] In other words, the narrow path is a journey, a lifestyle, one that is marked by characteristics of Christ, the gatekeeper. **And choosing the narrow path does not only bring eternal life, but it brings life and life abundantly—here and now!**

And in contrast, the wide gate, the one that everyone else is leaning toward leads to destruction, not just in the age to come, but here and now! Think about it. Take some time to consider some of your worst mistakes, your sins.

15. F. D. Bruner, *The Christbook: Matthew 1–12,* 2nd and rev. ed (W. B. Eerdmans Publishing Company, 2004), 350.

In what ways did these choices lead to destruction?

When I think about some of my sins, I can clearly see the path of destruction in my wake. When I think about my "smaller" sins—the ones that I still sometimes justify —I can also see how they too lead to destruction, even if they're more socially acceptable. When I spend more money than I had budgeted, it can show that my idolatrous heart is leaning toward materialism instead of kingdom-minded generosity and stewardship. When I am short tempered with my family after a sleep-deprived night, the world might say I'm justified *hashtagmomlife,* but I can see how my short words cause pain in my home.

The narrow way leads to life today and forever. And the wide path leads to destruction, both eternally and here and now. Our salvation has both eternal implications *and* present-day implications.

This isn't the prosperity gospel. This doesn't mean that if you do more for Jesus He'll bless you. What this means is that **the way of Jesus, the teachings of Jesus, and His wisdom for our lives is better than anything we can come up with ourselves**. And Christ not only saves us from eternal damnation, but He saves us from destruction *today.* The narrow way leads to goodness and mercy and life abundantly now, and in the age to come!

This is good news.

Read Matthew 7:15–20 and answer the questions below.

What does this passage say we're to look out for?

How will we know them?

In thinking about charisma, how can you tell if a person is being genuine or if they're being fake?

Have you ever planted a garden? I have, and I'm sad to report that nothing survived. As such, I will be giving you zero advice about plants in this Bible study. However, my father-in-law is a farmer. He mostly raises animals, but the past few years he's dabbled in strawberries and has a beautiful field in eastern North Carolina, where in the spring, his grandkids love to explore and eat fruit right off the plants.

The thing about strawberries is you can't plant them a week before you want the fruit. In the fall, a good farmer gets his field ready and starts planting and tending to these "berry" sensitive plants. Months later, after watering and protecting the plants from frost and harsh weather in the spring, a good farmer will often see the fruit of his or her labor.

In contrast, when I first started my garden, it looked so good! It had the appearance of garden with fresh soil, packets of seeds, and all the shiny new gear. And yet, a few months later, it yielded little to no fruit. Similarly, charisma can look like good character, but we can only tell the difference once we see the fruit.

The same can be said when evaluating preachers, teachers, and people who tickle our ears with charismatic messages. There are obvious situations where you can see what the fruit of a certain behavior—such as false teaching—will be; but many times, charisma can only keep up the façade for a short period of time. The fruit always tells the truth.

We read Matthew 23 in Week 1, but reread verses 1–12. How are these false teachers described?

Can you identify some potential false teachings in your life? Where do you hear them most? What are they loud about? What type of fruit are they producing?

For me, I am exposed to false teachings when I am not intentional about my time on social media. Many voices are loud about division and being "right in their own eyes," and ultimately, the fruit they produce often leads to further division and self-obsession.

Read Matthew 7:21–29 and answer the questions below.

In verses 21–29 we're given another comparison. Who is this passage comparing?

Look at verse 24 and circle the word "Therefore." Draw an arrow pointing to the verses above it. Summarize verses 21–23 in your own words below.

Reread Matthew 7:24 and fill in the blanks:

"Therefore, everyone who ________________ these words of mine and puts them into ______________________ is like a ______________ man . . ."

How is a wise man described in these verses?

How is a foolish man described?

Think about a wise woman or man in your life. Write their name down and then describe them. What are some of the characteristics or fruit you see in their lives?

Would you describe them as a man or woman of character, or simply a charismatic person? What's the difference?

Look up the verses below. Write a summary of what each one has to say about good character.

Proverbs 10:9

Titus 2:7–8

Proverbs 22:1

In light of what we've read and learned today and yesterday, what would it look like for *you* to choose character over charisma?

We're going to answer that question tomorrow, but I want you to preemptively think about your life and how you can do this today.

Prayer

In your life, what does it look like to choose character? What areas do you need to build your house on a sturdy foundation? Spend some time praying and asking the Holy Spirit to open your eyes and soften your heart to any area of your life that might need conviction and change.

Memory Verse

Read Colossians 3:2 and then try to fill in the blanks from memory below.

"Set your ________________ on ________________ ________________, not on ________________ ________________."

KEY TAKEAWAY: In the battle of character vs. charisma, we choose the narrow way of Jesus, and we build our lives on Him. *And* we look to the fruit to evaluate what leads to life and what leads to destruction.

WEEK 2 | **DAY 4**

A Woman of Character

Galatians 5:13–26

The last two days, we've talked about setting our hearts and minds on Christ (Day 2) and choosing the narrow way—Jesus! (Day 3). Today, we're going to ask the question, "What does a life of character look like?" If we believe that in Christ we are holy and deeply loved, and we're committed to choosing character over charisma, how do we actually live that out?

Let's jump into Scripture to see.

Read Galatians 5:13–18 and answer the questions below.

Who is the author of Galatians, Paul, talking to here?

Look at verse 13. As believers, we are called to be ____________, but our __________________________ shouldn't be to serve our selves, but to serve each other humbly in ____________.

Circle that last word you just wrote down (hint: the last word in verse 13). We're about to take a journey fleshing out this word that gets tossed around and said so easily. Before we do that, take a moment to summarize what you believe verse 14 means.

We're going to spend a moment looking up a few other passages to see what the whole Bible says about this love. The author of Galatians references this passage in verse 14, but let's start our journey looking at Matthew 22:36–40 ourselves.

In this passage, Jesus is being questioned by the Pharisees. They're trying to test His knowledge and set up a "gotcha moment," but Jesus doesn't play their games. In these verses, they ask Him to pick out the greatest commandment in all of the law. Let's look at Jesus' reply in verses 37–40.

What is the first and greatest commandment?

What is the second greatest commandment?

Read John 13:35. What does this verse say is the sign of a true disciple of Jesus?

Now read 1 Corinthians 13. How is this sign of a true disciple described in this passage? Fill in the columns below to answer this.

Love is . . .	Love does not . . .

In light of all of these verses on love, we can deduce that as followers of Jesus and the narrow way, we are to be a people who are known by our love. In the battle between character vs. charisma, our character *must* be rooted in love. Otherwise, our lives are just a clanging cymbal with only the appearance of good. Because love of God and love for others is not just one of the fruits we see in Jesus followers, they are the greatest laws that everything else we do flows from.

What does Galatians 5:16 say is the key to living a life of love instead of a life of destruction?

Verses 17–18 give us a picture of a battle between our flesh (what we want) and the Spirit (what God wants and what is for our ultimate good).

Verse 17 says that they are in ______________________ with each other so that you are not to do ____.

Think about a popular message in the world today that gives the opposite advice we see in verses 16–18; write the popular message below. What is the fruit of this type of messaging?

Read Galatians 5:19–24 and answer the questions below.

I recently heard my pastor teach on this passage, and something he said stood out to me: This passage isn't simply a list of dos and don'ts. This is so much more than that! These verses paint a picture of life with Christ and life apart from Christ.[16] But before we can fully understand this section of the passage, let's look again at the verses that come right before it.

---

16. Mike Ashcraft sermon series on faithfulness, Port City Church, Oct. 5 and Oct. 12, 2025.

Reread Galatians 5:16–18. In this passage, we're told to walk by the Spirit and to stay away from our fleshly desires. In verses 19–24, we see what the fruit of a life lived according to the flesh looks like, and then we're given a picture of what a life lived according to the Spirit looks like.

Look at verse 16, verse 18, and verse 25. Respectively, these verses say we should ______________ by the Spirit, ______________ by the Spirit, and that we should keep ________________________ with the Spirit.

Yes, we could take this passage and make it a behavioral modification list, but if we did that, we'd be missing the main point: Live a life connected to the Spirit *because*—as we've learned the last two days—the narrow way leads to *life* and the ways of the flesh lead to destruction. These verses give a clearer picture of what life and destruction look like.

In the columns below, list what a life lived in the flesh and a life lived in the Spirit look like (don't miss out on the acts of the flesh listed in verse 26).

Acts of the flesh	Fruit of the Spirit

I love the visual of producing fruit while walking with the Spirit. Turn to John 15:5–9. Jesus tells us that He is the true vine, and we are the branches; if we ______________ in Him (v. 5), we will bear much fruit. Now, consider these verses from John 15 in light of what we read in Galatians 5. Jesus doesn't say that if we follow the long list in Galatians 5 that we'll bear fruit. No, Galatians 5 is showing us the fruit of a life connected to the vine.

The answer isn't to do better, be better, and never make a mistake. It's to walk in the Spirit.

Look at John 15:9. What word do you see mentioned three times in that verse? Underline it, or write it below.

What is the command given in John 15:9? Write it below, and then circle the word "remain" and draw an arrow to the word "love."

If you're thinking about the last question in yesterday's study and wondering how to choose character over charisma and the narrow way over the wide way, there is only one answer: Live by the Spirit; be connected to the vine.

And from that journey your life will produce good fruit like love, joy, peace, patience, kindness, goodness, faithfulness, gentleness, and self-control.

But apart from Him, when we choose the wide path of listening to our flesh instead of the Spirit, we are destined to paths full of the sinfulness and the heartache we see in Galatians 5:19–21 and 26.

For the believer, character vs. charisma might sound trite or maybe even unimportant. But we are always in the process of becoming—and the question is, are we becoming people with character deeply rooted in Jesus? Or do we merely have the appearance of doing good, but we're ruled by our flesh (charisma)?

I can't answer that for you, but I know in my heart what I long for myself and for every person reading this study. Lord, may it be so.

Prayer

Write out your own prayer below or spend time praying this prayer.

God, thank You for being a God of love and goodness and life. Your Word invites me to live by the Spirit, but sometimes I don't know how to do that. God, hold me close and help me to walk in the Spirit and live a life guided by You. Help me to remain in Your love. God, give me the wisdom to care more about my character than charisma. Help me be more like You each day. Amen.

Memory Verse

Write Colossians 3:2 below, and then speak the words aloud three times, working from memory as best you can. Feel free to use your Bible as needed.

KEY TAKEAWAY: Character isn't found in a laundry list of things to do and things to stay away from; character is developed by walking with the Spirit and remaining in His love, and over time your life will produce good fruit from staying connected to the vine.

WEEK 2 | **DAY 5**

Reflection and Wrap-Up

Over the last four days we've learned:

- When our hearts and minds are set on Christ, it changes how we live our lives. It frees us from the pressures of chasing fame, the approval of others, success in our work and other areas, and it focuses our hearts on what matters most: being called holy and deeply loved by a good God.
- In the battle of character vs. charisma, we choose the narrow way of Jesus, and we build our lives on Him. And we look to the fruit to evaluate what leads to life and what leads to destruction.
- The answer to "How do I live a life of character?" isn't found in a laundry list of things to do and things to stay away from. Character is developed first by walking with the Spirit and then remaining in His love.

Like last week, today is a shorter day. Reread one or all of the passages we read this week and spend some time journaling below by using the provided prompts.

Passages from the week:
Colossians 3; Matthew 7:13–29; 1 Samuel 16

What is one theme or truth from Scripture that stood out to you the most this week?

Has anything from this week changed, challenged, or shaped your thinking, your actions, or beliefs? If so, how?

What is one idea or verse that has encouraged you that you'd like to carry with you?

In light of what I've learned this week, character, to me, means . . .

Finish the sentence: Because of Christ, I . . .

Memory Verse

Write Colossians 3:2 from memory, below. If you can't, no worries! Grace upon grace! Write it out using your Bible as a reference.

Prayer

Spend some time talking to God below. Take what you just reflected on and turn it into a prayer. Thank God for what He's shown you this week, and ask Him to help you carry it forward.

KEY TAKEAWAY: In the battle of character vs. charisma, we choose the narrow way of Jesus, and we build our lives on Him. We look to the fruit to evaluate what leads to life and what leads to destruction.

WEEK THREE

SERVICE vs. STAGES

Key passages for this week: Matthew 6:1–15; Colossians 3:18–4:2; Philippians 2

Introduction: We're All Striving for Stages

As a parent, one of the things I've loved discovering is what each child gravitates toward. It's a beautiful thing to see a child learn their own personality and embrace the ways that God has wired them. Some of our kids are drawn toward the stage. It's almost like a magnetic pull; they naturally thrive in a spotlight or when they're the center of attention, and it's clearly the way God designed them!

At the same time, I've learned that our kids, who would rather be just about anywhere other than the center of attention, still long for a stage, just a different type of stage. They light up when we see them, validate who they are, and affirm their giftings. Some of them long for the stage of success, and others for relational status.

I'm the same way. I actually don't like being on a stage or being the center of attention (which is odd for a teacher to say, but it's true). And yet, I find myself striving for various figurative stages. I want to be seen as "successful" in my work inside the home and outside of it. I don't want an award or public affirmation, but I often find myself striving for affirmation from stages I've created in my mind. In my head I have an ideal of what success should look like, but since culture's definition of success is always changing, this world can keep me constantly striving for things that don't matter.

Whether it's having an audience of one thousand or an audience of one, we all long for significance. Which isn't necessarily a bad thing! We're made to find our significance in Christ. However, Satan, who is seeking to distract and devour us, knows this and has created traps and temptations for us to find our significance on worldly "stages."

We're living in a world where platforms can be created in the palm of our hands with just one viral post. Look around you; it's not hard to find the hustlers, the *hashtaggirlbosses*, and the family that is keeping up with the Joneses. Some people are striving for fame, while others are striving for success in various fields, whether it's homemaking or being a CEO. Some of us find our identity in who we know and the type of friendships we have.

The opportunity to highlight ourselves isn't a new thing as we'll see in the passage this week. I think about the Pharisees that Jesus rebuked. They didn't have Instagram or TikTok, but their stage was one of self-righteousness and "right living." They loved highlighting how much better they were than others in their community.

Humanity has been building stages since the beginning of time, but our accessibility to the types of stages we long for has changed. And as easy as it is to point a finger at others on the internet or in our churches, this week I'd like for us to ask God to examine *our* hearts.

Stages are tricky. This week we're going to identify the stages that we're uniquely striving after, and how Scripture tells us that in the upside down ways of the kingdom of God, our significance is found in *Who* we belong to. And that belonging changes us so that we live lives of service for the kingdom—not service for our own tiny kingdoms we so often like to build. So, whether you're seeking significance in online stages, private stages, the stage of success at work or in your relationships, my prayer is that at the end of this week, you'll be able to find freedom from seeking stages and instead seek a life of service to a kingdom that cannot be shaken.

Big Picture Day

Thus far in the study we've learned that as believers who are learning to stop striving, we must choose...

Relationship instead of Religion (Week 1)

Character instead of Charisma (Week 2)

And this week we'll be learning to choose Service over Stages (Week 3).

Big Picture Questions

Today is our Big Picture day! Remember that each Day 1 focuses on Scripture. You will simply read and allow the passages to "marinate" before sinking your teeth into the text. Here are three guidelines as you begin each reading:

- Read the Scripture passages for the week in one sitting.
- Highlight any verses, words, or themes that stick out to you.
- In the margins, write any questions you might have as you read.

Consider how the verses relate to each other and to the overall theme of the week.

Read Matthew 6:1–15; Colossians 3:18–4:2; Philippians 2

Now answer each of the questions below:

What does this passage show me about God?

What does this passage show me about this world or humanity?

How does this passage apply to my life? Are there any principles that serve as a guide for the Christian life?

Read Psalm 139:23–24. Spend some time in prayer and ask God to show you the stages your heart longs for, and write them below. For example, one of my stages would be that I long to be seen as successful in my specific field, and I can often get distracted by striving for success instead of serving in other places God has called me. One of my friends' stages would be that she finds value in the types of friends she has, and she is often striving to maintain status or harmony in those relationships. *What about you? What stages are you striving after?*

Memory Verse

Read Colossians 3:1–2 and write the verses below.

> *"Since, then, you have been raised with Christ, set your hearts on things above, where Christ is, seated at the right hand of God. Set your minds on things above, not on earthly things."* Colossians 3:1–2

Prayer

Feel free to pray this prayer, or write out your own prayer to God below.

God, You are good. Would You bless my time this week studying Your word? Open my eyes to the riches of Your Word and don't let me walk away unchanged. Holy Spirit, move in my life, make my paths clear, and show me where in my life I'm striving for the stage. Jesus, help me walk away from this week knowing and loving You more.

WEEK 3 | **DAY 2**

Serving and Stages

Matthew 6:1–15

One of the most famous sermons in Scripture is Jesus' Sermon on the Mount. Matthew 6 is a part of this sermon, but it's not the beginning of it! In Matthew 5, Jesus starts this sermon with the beatitudes, and then He continues to share more wisdom for how we should live in this world. He contrasts what the world says with what the kingdom of God expects by using a phrase, "You have heard that it was said . . . but I tell you . . ."

For example, in Matthew 5:43–44, Jesus says: "***You have heard that it was said,*** 'Love your neighbor and hate your enemy.' ***But I tell you,*** love your enemies and pray for those who persecute you."

In other words, the world will tell you to love those whom it's easy to love and you're justified to hate your enemies; but in the kingdom of God, you're to love all people, even your enemies, even to the point that you will pray for those who wound you.

In the Sermon on the Mount, we're given quite a few "But I tell you" statements in order to paint a clear picture of what the world expects and what Christ followers should be doing instead. Our passage for Day 2 is a continuation of this wisdom.

In Matthew 6, Jesus gives us examples of what not to do, and then how we should live our lives instead. And yet, if you read the chapter in its entirety and only get a list of "to-do's" and "not to-do's," you've missed the heart behind His message. Jesus clearly wants His followers to serve others, but more than that, He's after our hearts.

Read Matthew 6:1 and answer the questions below.

This chapter starts out with a strong warning that serves as the thesis for the rest of the chapter. Write the warning in your own words below.

Why does verse 1 say that the Pharisees were practicing their good works and righteousness in front of others?

Look back at Matthew 5:14–16. Do you think the issue is practicing good works in front of others, or is there something deeper going on here? What do you think Jesus is actually getting at in Matthew 6:1?

As we learned earlier, Scripture tells us that God doesn't look at our outward appearances; instead, God knows and looks at our hearts (1 Sam. 16:7). In the kingdom of God, our motives matter. Why we do something is just as important as actually doing the thing God has called us to!

This is incredibly important because there are some of us whose very vocation is tied to a stage or doing good works in public. Maybe you're a performer, a minister, a nonprofit leader, or a public speaker. Maybe you're a doctor, nurse, a social worker, firefighter, or teacher, where your job is to do good for others in public! But the warning in verse 1 isn't about performing good works in front of others—it's about seeking a stage *in order to be seen* instead of serving from a stage in order to further kingdom work!

Can you see the difference? Reread verse 1 and underline the phrase "in order to be seen."

God isn't interested in the appearance of obeying Him; He requires full surrender. I once heard a pastor say, "It's way easier to pretend to be religious than to actually be surrendered." Let that sink in. We can have the appearance of obedience, but if our hearts, our motives, aren't in the right place . . .? That's just empty religion.

What's a surefire way to identify if you're surrendered or simply religious? Answer the question: ***Do I judge my performance based on the approval of others or am I committed to serving regardless of who is watching?***

Speaking of serving, let's keep reading.

Read Matthew 6:1–4 and answer the questions below.

In this passage, we're shown that we are supposed to serve the needy. In Matthew 5:13–16, we're called to be bright lights in a dark world. And serving others is actually assumed in the wording of these verses in Matthew 6. Notice that Scripture says, "When you give to the needy . . ." (vv. 2–3), not "If you give . . ." Serving others, and specifically in this passage "the needy," is an assumed part of the Christian life; it's not optional.

Look up these other passages; what do they say about serving the needy?

Deuteronomy 15:1–18

James 1:27

2 Corinthians 9:6–15

Galatians 2:10

What do you think is the purpose of service for those who follow Jesus?

Read 1 Peter 4:10–11, and answer that same question again: What does Scripture say about the purpose of service for those who follow Jesus?

Now turn back to Matthew 6:2–4. In verse 2, find the word used to describe the "stage seekers." Circle the word in your Bible, and keep an eye out for that word as we continue reading. In the space below, write the word and explain what comes to mind when you hear it.

According to Matthew 6:3, what is the purpose of service for the stage seekers described in this verse? How is it different from the purpose of service for those who follow Jesus?

In a world that invites us to share each and every good thing we do on the internet—our tiny personal stages—the way of Jesus invites us instead to a quiet, more meaningful life of service. To keep us from the temptation of doing things for others' praise, Jesus gives us a road map to freedom from striving!

Look at Matthew 6:3–4. What has Jesus told us to do in order for us to avoid sinning by making service about us and our personal stages?

Isn't it incredible? The God of the universe knows that we're prone to making service about ourselves, and He doesn't just tell us not to. He gives us the tools to stay away from the temptation of seeking the spotlight! You see, it's pretty difficult to be praised and honored by others when your service is performed in secret instead of on stages for the world to see.

Psalm 91:1–2 (NKJV) says, "He who dwells in the *secret place* of the Most High shall abide under the shadow of the Almighty. I will say of the LORD, 'He is my refuge and my fortress; My God, in Him I will trust.'"

The way for our striving to cease is to be so content with finding affirmation from our heavenly Father in the secret places that we are freed from needing affirmation in the public spaces. This frees us to *serve* freely without making it about us!

Based on what we've learned so far, let's rewrite Matthew 6:1–4 in modern language. Fill in the blank with words that either fit your life or fit our current space and time.

Beware, don't ____________________________________ in front of others in order to be praised from earthly stages. For when you're striving after stages and applause here on earth, you won't __________________________________. So when you ________________________, don't post on ________________, don't brag about it to your friends online or ______________________________. But when you honor those, you serve and honor God alone through your service, you don't need public applause. So let your service be done in secret, and ____________

____.

Read Matthew 6:5–15 and answer the questions below.

We learned what to do and what not to do from the hypocrites Jesus mentioned in the first section of Matthew 6, but in this second section, we're talking about prayer. Who else does Jesus tell us not to be like in verse 7?

Not just who, but how exactly *are they praying, and what is it about their prayers that we should avoid?*

I love the imagery from that language. One version of Scripture calls it "babbling like pagans" and another calls it "vain repetitions" (NKJV). We're not only supposed to stay away from boasting about our service and our faith from street corners, but *the way* we pray and talk about it in front of others matters too!

Look at verse 2 and then at verse 5. There are two reasons provided for why the hypocrites were serving others. List them below.

Scripture tells us that what's done in secret has its own reward. *Look at verses 4 and 6; what is the benefit of serving in secret instead of serving for recognition?*

Pause for a moment and think about your life. Where do you find yourself wanting to be seen and praised?

Read verses 9–13.

Once again, Jesus isn't just telling us to not do something and then leaving us alone to figure it out. He's given us a road map for how to not babble like the hypocrites who manage to make prayer a performance for their own reward. Verses 9–13 provide a sample prayer that we often refer to as the Lord's Prayer.

What do you notice about this prayer?

Let's look at the verses again. Who is the passage centered around?

If you had to summarize this prayer in your own words, what ultimately is it about?

Although Scripture doesn't give us the exact prayers that the hypocrites were praying, it does tell us about their motives. We can make some strong assumptions that the purpose of their prayers wasn't to talk to God or point to the character of God. Their prayers were designed to make *them* look good instead of making much of the One they were praying to. Think about that for a minute. *How many of your spiritual practices are about making much of Jesus? And how many are about striving for stages or affirmation in all the wrong places?*

At the end of the prayer, Jesus clarifies one specific topic within the prayer: forgiveness. Why do you think He focuses on this?

One thing about hypocrites, they often have high standards for others while making loopholes or exceptions for themselves. The Pharisees in the New Testament were notorious for telling others how to live their lives, and their capacity for showing grace was small. Yet their opinions of themselves were awfully high.

Read John 8:1–11 for another example of this hypocrisy.

Jesus reminds the hypocrites that forgiveness is for *all of us*, and all of us have been on the receiving end of it and should be quick to grant forgiveness.

In light of John 8 and Matthew 6:14–15, why is forgiving others so important?

Is there someone whom you've had trouble forgiving? If so, what next steps do you need to take in order to pursue forgiving them?

Today you've done a deep dive into Matthew 6:1–15, so let's come back up for some air and look at the big picture again. In this passage, we are given two ways that kingdom-minded people should live out their faith.

What are those two things?

Jesus is clear that it's not just about our behaviors, He is after our hearts as well. So not only should we be doing those two things, but we should be doing them in ______________________________, so that we're not tempted to make stages out of our service.

Memory Verse

Read Colossians 3:1–2, and then try your best to fill in the blanks from memory below (but remember, it's okay if you need to look back at Scripture!).

"Since, __________, you have been raised with _____________, set your _____________ on things above, where _____________ is, seated at the right hand of _____________. Set your _____________ on things above, not on earthly things."

Prayer

Spend a few moments asking God to bring to light any areas of your life where you're striving to be seen. Write them below and spend time praying over them and asking God to help you find your affirmation in Him.

KEY TAKEAWAY: Jesus wants your heart. And the way for your striving to cease is to be so content with finding affirmation from your heavenly Father in the secret places that we are freed from needing affirmation in the public spaces. This frees us to *serve* freely without making it about us!

Serving unto the Lord

Colossians 1:1–14; 3:18–4:2

Did you read today's passage and immediately get nervous toward the end? It's okay if so, because I must confess that I opened my Bible, looked at the passage, and said, "Help me be faithful, Jesus." You see, in some circles, some of these verses have been cherry-picked and used to abuse power and manipulate victims, and I want to be very gentle with you if that's you. I offer a specific invitation for you to come and sit with the words of Scripture and remember that we serve a loving God who is always working for our ultimate good (and His glory!).

With that said, we're going to look at today's passage in Colossians through the lens of serving God and serving others. Like all of our other sessions, today's lesson isn't a behavior modification study; I'm not going to try to intellectually force you into submission. This is what sets Christianity apart from many other religions and cults: **God isn't solely after behavior change. He offers a relationship with the one true God! And this gift is offered *freely*.** So, rest easy, dear one, if today's reading made you a bit nervous.

Last week we read Colossians 3:1–17, and we cannot explore the verses that follow without looking back at what we learned. If we consider our passage today on its own, it still has worth and is valid, *but* these words were penned together.

Our key takeaway for Day 2 was: When our hearts and minds are set on Christ, it changes how we live our lives. It frees us from the pressures of chasing fame, others' approval, success in our work, etc., and it focuses our hearts on what matters most: being called holy and deeply loved by a good God.

Today, we're going to take that one step further and build on that as we wrestle with the choice between chasing stages or living a life of service. For the Christian, our service to others is ultimately service to God. Whether we're teachers, mothers, writers, doctors, lawyers, janitors, cashiers, or chefs. Whatever role we have in life, we are called to "work at it with all your heart as working for Lord, not for human masters" (Col. 3:23).

And the passages today aren't merely prescriptive for specific people; but they're descriptive for how *everyone* should be choosing a life of serving others.

Let's dive in, beginning in Colossians, chapter 1.

Read Colossians 1:1–14 and answer the questions below.

We've talked about this already, but as a refresher, who wrote the book of Colossians, and who was he writing to?

What is Paul's tone in these verses?

After reading this section of this epistle, how would you describe the church in Colossae?

This is vital to keep in mind as we continue because Paul is talking to a group of people who are bearing good fruit! Paul isn't writing to reprimand these people; no, he's writing to edify and encourage. The church was not perfect, as Paul was teaching them about the supremacy of Christ and how that impacts their lives. But these were fellow believers!

Look at verses 10 and 11. What is Paul praying for and working toward?

That the recipients of his letter would "______________ a life ______________________ of the Lord and _________________ him in every way: bearing ____________________ in every good work, ____________________ in the ______________________ of God."

Why is Paul praying for and working toward this (vv 11–13)?

Paul has written an encouraging letter, one that serves as a reminder that Jesus Christ is Lord and He alone is sufficient. As a result, we too should live differently because of our salvation in Christ.

As we continue into Colossians 3, it is important that this tone and understanding is at the forefront of our minds.

Read Colossians 3:18–4:2 and answer the questions below.

Notice, Paul is casting a wide net here. Which groups of people does he mention?

These instructions are not for just anyone! They're for the Christian household. These instructions are for the good of the Christian family unit.

Before we go any further, it is imperative to note, especially in our specific context, that the type of slave and master relationship described in this passage is not the same type of chattel slavery that existed in America. The type of slavery that Paul is most likely referring to was a bond servant type of master/slave relationship. In this type of master/slave relationship, people could work to pay off their debts, or they could willingly work for a household for a season and then move on to another job as they pleased. Paul was not discussing widespread, race-based kidnapping and displacement of humans like we have experienced in our country's history. Paul is writing in a different context, and as a result, this passage should never be used as an argument for such inhumane treatment of people.

With that said, the culture that Paul is writing in still had many flaws (much like any culture this side of glory!). Its treatment of women as property and treatment of people at the margins was atrocious. And yet the gospel was transforming these systems from the inside out. Paul's words here aren't to support cultural bias and control, nor are they about slavery or equal rights under the law. No! They're actually written to encourage a way of living that Christian households should practice that aligns with the understanding that all are welcome at the foot of the cross because Christ reigns supreme. He's writing this so that Christians will run their households in a way that reflects God's economy instead of the world's.

Go back and read the verses right before this passage, Colossians 3:11–14, again and fill in the blanks below.

"Here there is _______ Gentile or Jew, circumcised or uncircumcised, barbarian, Scythian, slave or free, but _________________ is _______, and is in _______." (v. 11)

We use all of Scripture to interpret Scripture, so let's also look at some of Paul's words in Galatians 3:26–29 and see what he has to say about these categories that some were using (and still use) to separate and divide us.

> *"So in Christ Jesus you are all children of God through faith, For all of you who were baptized into Christ have clothed yourselves with Christ. There is neither Jew nor Gentile, neither slave nor free, nor is there male and female, for you are all one in Christ Jesus. If you belong to Christ, then you are Abraham's seed, and heirs according to the promise."* GALATIANS 3:26–29

In Christ we are all equal at the foot of the cross. Amen? Amen.

With that in mind, we can confidently examine the passage today through the lens of unity. If we're all one in Jesus, then what Paul is encouraging here is a life of radical service, living out the greatest commandments of loving God and others more than ourselves.

Through the lens of unity, radical love, and service, let's look at Colossians 3:18–4:2 again. There are six groups of people mentioned in these passages. Below, list the ways we might be tempted to use each of these positions within the household as a stage for ourselves instead of serving for others:

Wives *E.g., The world says that being a trophy wife can be our ultimate goal. The richer the husband, the better the life. Make a home insta-perfect and enviable. Bash your man on girls' nights, and show you really rule the roost!*	**Husbands**
Children	**Fathers**
Slaves	**Masters**

The gospel is countercultural; it's radical. What do these verses say about these roles?

Wives	**Husbands**
Children	**Fathers**
Slaves	**Masters**

What differences do you notice between the two lists?

Read Colossians 3:5–17, the verses that come right before this passage. Notice the beautiful world and relationships that Paul is describing. Underline verse 11 in your Bible. Below, list again the descriptors of God's chosen people in verses 12–15.

You see, Paul is speaking to a specific context, and within those societal frameworks, he's calling believers to care about how they work, how they serve, and how they treat the people God has placed in their lives. And specifically, in the context of the Christian household, Paul uses the various unique roles people have to display the Christian work ethic of service and putting others before themselves.

Those characteristics listed in Colossians 3:12–15 provide the context in which submission (v. 18), love (v. 19), obedience (v. 20, 22), gentleness (v. 21), and service (vv. 21–23) take place. There, service can grow and selfishness can be put to death.

Look at Colossians 3:23–24. Who are we working for?

For the Christian, our service to others is ultimately service to God. Whether we're teachers, mothers, writers, doctors, lawyers, janitors, cashiers, or chefs. Whatever place we have in life, we are called to "work at it with _____ _________ ____________, as working for ______ ___________, not for human masters."

Is it natural for you to serve others? Why or why not?

Memory Verse

Read Colossians 3:1–2 and then try to fill in the blanks from memory below.

"Since, ________, you have ________ ____________with __________,
set your ________ on things ____________, where ____________ is,
______________ at the ____________ hand of ____________.
Set your ________ on things ____________, not on ____________ things."

Prayer

Ask the Lord to lead you to places where you can serve and work for His glory.

KEY TAKEAWAY: Our key takeaway from Colossians last week was this: When our hearts and minds are set on Christ, it changes how we live our lives. It frees us from the pressures of chasing fame, others' approval, success in our work, etc., and it focuses our hearts on what matters most: being called holy and deeply loved by a good God. And this week we're building on that by adding: That good news frees us from a life of making it all about us, while inviting us to a life of radical service and love in the spaces and places God has called us.

WEEK 3 | **DAY 4**

Humble Service

Philippians 2:1–11

When my husband and I started the adoption process for our first son, we were very well-intentioned, but we were also young and clueless (an understatement). And yet, we felt strongly that our family was called to be the hands and feet of Jesus here on earth, and one of the ways we were uniquely called to live that out was by opening our home and our lives to children in need.

Along the way, we noticed a few things that didn't line up with our core values. At the beginning of our journey, we met some people and organizations who believed that the purpose of adoption was to find the perfect child for the family; but the more we learned about adoption, the more we believed that the purpose of adoption was to find a safe family for every child.

The first centers on the wants of the parents, and the second centers on the needs and well-being of the child.

We started partnering with a Christian organization that guided us through a more biblical and "others-centered" approach to adoption. The goal wasn't for every family to find the perfect child, but for every child to have a safe and loving family that was equipped to meet their unique needs. This intention kept our family from making adoption about us.

Our passage today highlights the subtle difference between these approaches, explaining what a life of service looks like. And it encourages us not to get our intentions twisted: Even in our good deeds, we're not to make *anything* about us.

Read Philippians 2:1–4 and answer the questions below.

In the first verse, what words or ideas are repeated? Underline them in your Bible and write them below.

An "if/then" statement is a conditional sentence that connects one idea to a specific, often logical, outcome: "If it snows, then it must be cold outside." Verses 1–4 follow a similar pattern.

Circle all the "Ifs" and "Thens" in in these verses.

Write the four "If/then" statements below.

1.

2.

3.

4.

Paul is saying, "*If* you are one of God's children, united into His family, redeemed by His love, and equipped by the Holy Spirit to live a life of tenderness and compassion, *then* the following verses hold the logical outcome of how you should live! This is what a life worthy of the gospel of Jesus looks like.

If you've been saved by grace through faith, ***then*** your life will be changed.

How exactly has your life changed? I thought you'd never ask. Let's take a look at what comes after "then." Note the six actions Paul commands believers to take:

Make my joy complete by being (1) ____________________, (2) having the ________ __________, (3) being one in ______________ and of one ________. (4) Do __________ out of __________ ____________ or vain conceit. Rather, in humility (5) ________ __________ above yourselves,

(6) not looking to your own ______________ but each of you to the ______________ of _______ ________________.

Look at Philippians 2:1 again and you'll find the subtle difference between behavior modification and a life transformed by the good news of Jesus.

Behavior modification only deals with outward actions. Changing certain behaviors looks good, but it only deals with the surface, and it often comes up lacking as it keeps us striving after short-term change instead of long-term impact! Behavior modification says: *Check all of these boxes in order to please God.* But the gospel says: *Experience a saving love like no other, and you can't help but walk away changed by it.*

The world says do more and be more and maybe you can earn your standing in society or with God. But Scripture says, that ***if*** you are united in Christ, comforted by His redeeming love, ***then*** you should live a life of unity within the body of Christ, doing nothing out of selfish ambition, but serving others and putting their interests above your own.

This is what a true believer looks like and why we are told throughout Scripture that **the world looks on the outside, but God cares about our hearts.** It's possible to change your behavior and pursue unity, service, and selflessness; that's why many of us have friends and coworkers who are kind and generous people (common grace!) but don't know Jesus.

This passage isn't saying do better or be better. It's saying, because of Christ's love for you and through you, your life will change.[17] It mostly likely won't change overnight, but through sanctification (which happens in community and through studying His Word), you will become more like Him each day.

A natural next question might be, "Awesome, Brittany. I want that change in my life, but *how* exactly do I make that happen?"

This is one of the complexities and mysteries of faith that I will never fully understand, but our reading today does point us in a specific direction.

---

17. 1 Samuel 16:7; Jeremiah 17:10; Psalm 139:23; Proverbs 21:2.

Read Philippians 2:5–8 and answer the questions below.

Who are we to look to as an example of how to live?

When considering how we serve God and others, we must have the same mindset as

____________________.

That sounds daunting! Jesus Christ "made himself nothing" (Phil. 2:7), came to earth as a baby, lived a perfect life of service and teaching, and then died a gruesome death and overcame evil and darkness through His resurrecting power. Wow, that is a tall order.

Because of Christ, we are not called to live this out perfectly. He came to earth *because* we are flawed! He knew we couldn't pull this off alone. And yet, our calling to "be holy, as Christ is holy" remains.[18]

In Philippians 2:6–8, identify the various mindsets of Jesus Christ, and write them out in the space provided below.

18. 1 Peter 1:15–16.

Read Philippians 2:9–11 and answer the questions below.

According to these verses, what was the purpose of Jesus' life of service?

Looking at verses 10–11, what should then be the purpose of our life of service as well?

Considering verses 9–11, describe what you think a life of service looks like for the believer.

One of the things that stands out to me in this passage is the phrase, "do nothing." Circle that phrase, and above it write the words, "No good deed, no ministry, nothing.*"*

I love how in a passage on humility and service, we are reminded to not do *anything* for selfish reasons. My human heart has a way of making even good things about me. Like I mentioned earlier, we were even tempted to make adoption more about us and our needs instead of the needs of a child and their first family. That's embarrassing for me to write, but praise God that He didn't leave me there! He brought in fellow believers to help me see His heart in adoption, and throughout that process, He changed mine.

It's easy for our hearts to start making our lives, our work, our ministries, even our volunteering about us! What starts as a genuine attempt to partner with God in His kingdom work can quickly turn ugly. But God in His goodness doesn't leave our hearts alone; **no corners of our hearts can be kept hidden from His redeeming love**.

We get to be grateful that even in serving others and practicing good deeds, because of Jesus, we have nothing to prove and nothing to earn. So, we show up humbly, committed to unity in the body of Christ and serving others selflessly.

Memory Verse

Fill in the blanks below with the words from Colossians 3:1–2.

Since, then, ______ ________ ________ _____________ ________ ____________,

set your __________ ____ _____________ ______________ where _____________

is, ____________ _____ ______ ____________ ___________ of God. ____ _______

__________ ____ things above, _____ ____ ____________ ___________.

Prayer

Are there any good deeds or areas of service in which you've slowly lost sight of the end goal (Phil. 2:10–11) and have started to make it about you? If so, spend some time confessing that below and asking the Lord to change your heart. If not, ask God to search your heart and show you if there is any selfish ambition distracting you from living on mission.

KEY TAKEAWAY: *If* we are united with Christ, *then* we are called to lives of unity and service, doing *nothing* out of selfish ambition, but in humility valuing others above ourselves (just as Christ did for us when He gave His life for us).

Reflection and Wrap-Up

Over the last four days we've learned:

- Jesus wants our hearts. And the way for our strivings to cease is to be so content with finding affirmation from our heavenly Father in the secret places that we are freed from needing affirmation in the public spaces. This frees us to *serve* freely without making it about us!
- The good news of Jesus frees us from a life of making it all about us, while inviting us to a life of radical service and love in the spaces and places God has called us.
- *If we are united with Christ, then we are called to lives of unity and service, doing nothing out of selfish ambition, but in humility valuing others above ourselves (just as Christ did for us when He gave His life for us).*

It's Day 5! Today is a shorter day. Reread one or all of the passages we read this week and spend some time journaling below by using the provided prompts.

Passages from the week:
Matthew 6:1–15; Colossians 3:18–4:2; Philippians 2

What is one theme or truth from Scripture that stood out to you the most this week?

Has anything from this week changed, challenged, or shaped your thinking, your actions, or beliefs? If so, how so?

What is one idea or verse that has encouraged you that you'd like to carry with you?

In light of what I've learned this week, true service, to me, means . . .

Finish the sentence: Because of Christ, I . . .

Memory Verse

Write Colossians 3:1–2 from memory below. If you can't, no worries! Grace upon grace! Write it out using your Bible as a reference.

Prayer

Spend some time talking to God. Take what you just reflected on and turn it into a prayer and write it below. Thank God for what He's shown you this week, and ask Him to help you carry it forward.

KEY TAKEAWAY: In the battle of service vs. stages, we remember that Jesus is after our hearts and this changes *everything*. Because of this we serve joyfully, without making it about us, because we are united in Christ and share in His mindset, valuing the well-being of others above ourselves.

Key passages for this week: Acts 2:42–47 and Romans 12:3–18; Luke 15:11–24 and Ecclesiastes 4:7–12

Introduction: Made to Belong

Almost a decade ago, my husband and I moved away from our deeply loved community in North Carolina and moved to West Texas. We were far from family and didn't know a soul. For a few weeks, I loved walking into Target not knowing anyone, completely uninterrupted to accomplish my tasks. I could have walked in wearing my pajamas and not a single person would have taken notice (and if you're wondering if I did, you should know that at the time I had three kids aged three and under, so yes I did leave my house in pj's).

Rather quickly, the newness of anonymity wore off as isolation became a heavy burden. I remember filling out paperwork for a new pediatrician's office and having to leave an emergency contact blank because we hadn't found our people yet. When holidays or birthdays came around, we realized quickly that not having family or close friends nearby was hard. Our marriage's health and our spiritual health were directly impacted by our extreme seclusion.

And so, we threw ourselves into building a robust community in our new town. We invited people into our home and joined a local church. We met neighbors and said yes to just about every invitation we received. And years later, when we left that little town to come back home to North Carolina,

I was just crushed because we had grown to love and be loved by such a beautiful community. We weren't leaving behind acquaintances, but people who had become spiritual brothers and sisters in Christ, and friends who were like family.

This example of us moving is a surface-level example of a spiritual issue going on: **We were made for community**—from the beginning of creation when God said it wasn't good for man to be alone, until the last book of the Bible where we see God's people *together* from every tribe, nation, and tongue. It is clear we serve a God whose very design is for His people to be a part of something greater than themselves! Part of becoming a Christian is belonging to the family of God. And this belonging is how we grow in godliness, and it serves as protection from falling into patterns of sin (like striving).

This week, we will be wrestling with God's design for community, the dangers of isolation and hyper-independence, and lastly, the blessing of belonging.

WEEK 4 | **DAY 1**

Big Picture Day

Thus far in the study we've learned that as believers who are learning to stop striving, we must choose . . .

Relationship instead of Religion (Week 1)

Character instead of Charisma (Week 2)

Service instead of Stages (Week 3)

And this week we'll be learning to choose Community instead of Isolation (Week 4).

Big Picture Questions

Today is our Big Picture day! Remember that each Day 1 focuses on Scripture. You will simply read and allow the passages to "marinate" before sinking your teeth into the text. Here are three guidelines as you begin each reading:

- Read the Scripture passages for the week in one sitting.
- Highlight any verses, words, or themes that stick out to you.
- In the margins, write any questions you might have as you read.

Consider how the verses relate to each other and to the overall theme of the week.

Read Acts 2:42–47 and Romans 12:3–18; Luke 15:11–24 and Ecclesiastes 4:7–12.

Now answer each of the questions below:

What does this passage show you about God?

What does this passage show you about this world or humanity?

How does this passage apply to your life? Are there any principles that serve as a guide for the Christian life?

Memory Verse

Refresh your memorization of Colossians 3:1–2, and then read this week's memory verse, Colossians 3:3, and write it below.

> *"For you died, and your life is now hidden with Christ in God."* COLOSSIANS 3:3

Prayer

Feel free to pray this prayer, or write out your own prayer to God below.

God, thank You for the gift of Your Son, Jesus. And thank You for the gift of being in a real relationship with You and becoming a part of Your family. God, this week as I explore what it looks like to choose community instead of isolation, will You help me release any earthly expectations that aren't from You? And will You help me build a better framework for what it looks like to be connected to the body of Christ? In Jesus' name, amen.

WEEK 4 | DAY 2

God's Good Design

Acts 2:42–47; Romans 12:3–18

One of the things I'll never get over is the incarnation, the coming of Jesus Christ. I'll never get over how the God of the universe decided that His rescue plan would include coming to earth as a human, a tiny baby birthed in a manger to a virgin mother. The Son of God lived and breathed and walked among us. He laughed, He cried, He had friends. He ate meals and went on walks, and instead of overthrowing a corrupt government, He died and overcame the grave so that He could overcome *all* death and corruption once and for all.

I don't understand it, because if I were God I wouldn't come down in the most unassuming way. I would be riding chariots of fire down from the heavens with a slew of angels blasting music from their horns. The world would not be able to miss my entrance. And if I were God of the universe, I would for sure skip the toddler and infant years when I would be dependent on another human for my very life's existence.

And yet, the God of this world came close so that you and I could be a part of His family. Not only that, He didn't come down and live a life of solitude! He had twelve disciples and many friends. I think of how He spoke to Mary and Martha, and how He wept for his friend Lazarus. Jesus, our good news, lived in community with people. He modeled how we should love and care for those around us. **Community and belonging are a part of the DNA of God's good design for His people.** And Jesus modeled that from the time He was born, until His ascension into heaven.

When reading the whole of Scripture, you cannot miss the theme of belonging to a communal people of God. We don't have time this week to explore that whole storyline, but today we're going to look at two passages of Scripture that show us what God's good design for a community of believers should look like.

Read Acts 2:42–47 and answer the questions below.

My Bible titles this section the "Fellowship of the Believers," but these verses simply describe what the new church looked like after Pentecost when Jesus ascended into heaven and the Holy Spirit descended upon God's people. During this time, Peter delivered a sermon and thousands of people joined the family of God and community of believers! These verses we're reading today describe how these communities lived. The church in Acts 2 is held up as a prime example of how Christian communities *should* live.

In verse 42, we see that the believers devoted themselves to four things. List them below.

1.

2.

3.

4.

In our modern-day setting, what would it look like for you to devote yourself to the same things? In each of the items you listed above, describe how it would look to be devoted to them in your everyday life.

1.

2.

3.

4.

In verse 44, it says that "all of the believers were ______________________________

and had ______________________________ in common."

What do you think this means? (Hint: What this doesn't mean is that they all had the same favorite color and they all agreed on what was the best meal to cook that night. Look at verses 45–47 for further clarity.)

While the world says you and you alone are responsible for yourself, what do these passages say in contrast?

Does this radical type of belonging excite or terrify you, and why? (It's okay, be real here! If I'm being honest, it makes me and my independent American spirit a bit nervous while also excited about this radical belonging).

Look up the following passages. What do each say about God's design for community?

Hebrews 10:24–25

Galatians 6:2

Read Romans 12:3–8 and answer the questions below.

Earlier in the study, we learned to choose service over stages, laying down our pride and ego. In this passage, we read something similar. Verse 3 echoes what we learned in Week 2:

"Do not think of yourself __________ ______________ than you ought, but rather think of yourself with _______________ ____________________."

Notice the word "for" in verse 4? I was once told in a Bible class that oftentimes when you see the word "for" in Scripture it's there to tell you what or why the previous statement is there for. (See what I did there)? According to verses 4–8, why are we told to not think highly of ourselves?

You see, the world will tell you to either think highly of yourself in order to find your worth *or* the world will promote a false humility where you hide your worth behind a façade in order to meet a social norm. Both ways end up focusing on the outcome for the individual and ultimately lead to more striving. But Scripture says, **you belong to God, so you have a rightful place and role among the people of God.** Don't think too highly of yourself because we all have been given different gifts and we are called to steward them for the kingdom—not ourselves.

Verse 5 says that we're all a part of one body, belonging to one another, but we all have different roles.

In your Bible, underline the word "belongs." Next, read Romans 12:9–21 and answer the questions below. Looking at this passage, we see a few imperative verbs (meaning the apostle Paul is telling believers what is expected of them).

On the drawing below, list the commands that the body of Christ should be following.

Out of the commands mentioned above, which ones come easily to you in the context of community?

On the flip side, which of these are harder?

What I love about this is that we have one body but many parts! If you're not naturally adept in some of these areas, that's okay. Team up with someone in your real live community who is and learn from them. And if you're just killing it in the hospitality department or another area, fantastic! Bring along others in that journey and play your part to fill the gaps in the body of Christ.

In the very last verse, Paul is speaking to this one body full of many parts and tells them to not be overcome by evil, but to overcome evil with what?

Isn't that a beautiful picture?

I don't know about you, but I still have the tendency to read this as an individual. All of those commands to live united, practice hospitality, bless those who curse you —none of these can be done while flying solo! Trust me, I've tried. But something powerful happens when we come together, united in our sincere love for God and for others. **Together, living united and spurring each other on to good works, we can overcome evil with good.**

This is God's good design for community!

Sister, we're not called to do this Christian life alone. And I know it's hard with our busy schedules and our crazy jobs and demanding families; prioritizing community can always feel like it should be set on the back burner. But if you're a Christian, you're called to be an active part of the body of Christ. One body. Many parts. And you belong and have a unique role to play.

We need you. And you need us.

Look back at Acts 2. What's the very last sentence in the chapter? Write it below.

The beauty of belonging is that our connectedness and shared dependency on Christ ultimately help us overcome evil with good—not just in our own lives, but in our homes, our workplaces, our neighborhoods, and our churches. And ultimately, like the people of God in Acts 2, **when we live radically, other lives are changed and more people are added to the body of Christ as a result!**

Lord, let it be so.

Memory Verse

Read Colossians 3:3 and then try your best to fill in the blanks from memory below (but remember, it's okay if you need to look back at Scripture!).

"For you ___________, and your ___________ is now hidden with _______________ in ___________."

Prayer

Spend some time talking to God about how you feel about the idea of community and belonging to the family of God. Bring to Him any specific prayer requests you have about your community.

KEY TAKEAWAY: What a gift it is to belong to the family of God (One body. Many parts!), where our connectedness and shared dependency on Christ ultimately help us overcome evil with good—not just in our own lives, but in our homes, our workplaces, and our communities.

WEEK 4 | **DAY 3**

The Danger of Isolation

Luke 15:11–24; Ecclesiastes 4:7–12

When I was growing up there was a secular song that I loved to blast in my car, with the windows down and the volume up. It was by a trio of women and was a rally cry for independent women, celebrating their ability to make their own money and buy their own things.

Now, please note that as most young teenagers do, I didn't understand half of what I was singing. But as a sixteen-year-old who was making minimum wage at the local Bath & Body Works, I for sure classified myself as an independent woman even though I still needed my parents' help to finance most, if not all, areas of my life.

It's okay, you can laugh.

And yet, this song was my jam. It is the perfect picture of the cultural movement I grew up in. During my teenage years and young adulthood, being an independent woman was something to aspire to. And as I went to college and grad school, becoming a "boss babe" or something of the sorts, was in vogue.

But more than that, my American culture values independence, self-reliance, and personal freedom. These cultural values are a part of the makeup of our country. They aren't necessarily a good or a bad thing. There are a number of reasons why those characteristics can be extremely beneficial to a society. However, unchecked, they can also cause harm.

Extreme independence can lead to isolation.

Extreme self-reliance can lead to pride and exclusion.

And extreme personal freedom can lead to a selfishness that doesn't consider the needs or well-being of others.

And extreme isolation can often lead to striving after the wrong things when we remove ourselves from the edification and input that Christian community provides.

Yesterday we talked about how it's God's good design for us to be in community, but today we're going to talk about the danger of isolation and why it can be hard for some of us to belong—truly belong—to community.

Read Luke 15:11–24 and answer the questions below.

Right off the bat, the stage is set. We have two brothers who are set to inherit money and assets from their father. What does the younger brother do?

Look at verse 13. Beyond just asking for his share, what did he do?

Here's the thing about sin. Satan doesn't just want us to make a mistake, he wants to use sin to isolate and trap you. Notice: It wasn't enough for the younger son to simply be greedy and spend his inheritance. Sin separated him from his family. He went off on his own. He was alone. And although initially I'm sure he had a blast spending his inheritance, sin always takes us farther than we expected to go—and oftentimes it takes us farther from our community as well.

Read vv. 14–16, where did the young son's sin and isolation lead him?

Proverbs 18:1 (CSB) says:

> *"One who isolates himself pursues selfish desires;*
> *he rebels against all sound wisdom."* PROVERBS 18:1 (CSB)

Draw an arrow from the words "isolates himself" to "selfish desires." Then draw an arrow from the word "rebels" to "sound wisdom."

This is exactly what the younger son did. He isolated himself so he could pursue selfish desires. He rebelled and rejected sound wisdom. And he found himself in a literal pigsty, starving and alone.

Have you ever found yourself in a figurative pigsty? Has there ever been a time in your life where you isolated yourself and pursued selfish desires, rebelling against all sound wisdom? If so, how did that turn out for you?

Listen, if what you wrote above brought on feelings of shame, I want you to know this: We have *all* rebelled in some form or fashion according to Romans 3:23, but there is *no* shame or condemnation for those who are in Christ Jesus. Jesus paid it all, and like the good father in this story, He loves it when His children come home. We're not visiting the past to shame ourselves; we're visiting the past to learn from it and to keep ourselves from isolation.

Look at Luke 15:17. It says, "When he came to his senses . . ." Phew! That's a whole sermon in one tiny phrase because at one point, praise God, the Holy Spirit awakens each of us and brings us to our senses!

But notice what comes after that. What is the first thing the young son takes note of? (Second half of v. 17.)

His first observation was one of belonging.

He noted that even the outsiders who belonged in his father's community were better cared for than what he was experiencing out on his own. He'd rather be even distantly connected to his father's house—even as hired help—than starving and alone, living in a distant land.

Look at v. 21. The son tells the father, "Father, I have ____________________ against heaven and against you. I am ______ ___________________ ____________________ to be called your son."

Make no mistake, beloved. Sin's goal is always to separate you from communion and right relationship with God and others. The son says the hard part aloud: I've sinned. I've messed up. And because I've chosen isolation and darkness and debauchery, I'm not worthy of carrying the name of this family any longer. I'm not worthy of belonging.

And yet the good father in the story does what (vv. 22–24)?

Notice the wording in v. 24: "'For this son of mine was ____________________ and is ____________________ again; he was _______________ and is _________________.' So they began to celebrate."

You see isolation leads to death and being lost, but belonging leads to life and being found.

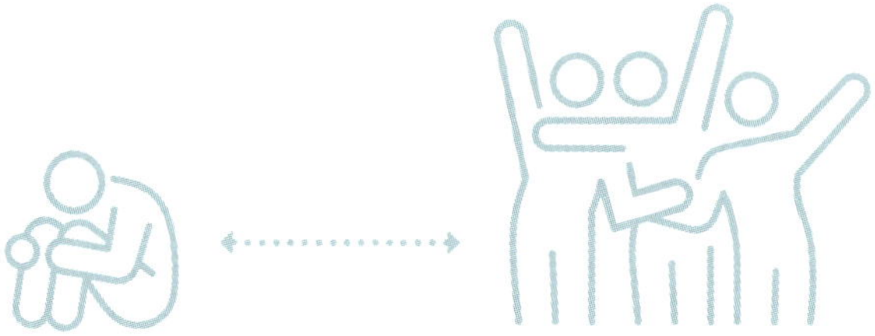

This story of the prodigal son is a parable that points us to the ultimate Father who has made a way for you and me to belong to His family, even though at one point we were lost and isolated and choosing our own way. The cross is the ultimate bridge from isolation to belonging.

Read Ecclesiastes 4:8–12 and answer the questions below.

What are the dangers of isolation in this passage?

And in contrast, what are the benefits listed in this passage?

Take a moment and look at your own life. You know yourself better than anyone else! What are the lies that tempt you toward isolation?

For me, one lie is that it's easier to do things on my own. I asked a friend that question and she said it would be that if people got to know the real her, then maybe they wouldn't like her or they'd be disappointed.

What are the potential dangers of isolation in your own life?

Tomorrow we'll be discussing the blessing of community, but let's go ahead and prime the pump a bit. What are the current or potential blessings of belonging in your life?

I want to take a moment and acknowledge that some of us are in seasons where we're rarely alone and we desperately need some moments of solitude (I currently have six kids in my house as I'm writing this. As I wrote this sentence, I had to stop because the toddler fell and was crying, and the dogs were barking at the mailman. I get you, sister). This study isn't anti-alone time! Jesus went off to pray by Himself, but He also returned to His disciples (even if they were sleeping) and He lived a life on mission, loving and serving people everywhere He went. There are many good things about the practice of solitude, especially when you belong to the body of Christ.

The point of today is that **if you're a Christian, you're called to a life of belonging. Resisting this calling is often evidence of striving to handle life on your own!** You're a part of a family (one body, many parts). And you cannot belong and be a part of a family if you isolate yourself. And the danger of isolation is getting separated from the community that helps you stay connected to your truest identity and calling.

Let's end on an encouraging note, reminding ourselves of that truth. Flip to Hebrews 10:23–25 and fill in the blanks below.

"Let us hold ______________________________ to the hope we profess, for he who promised is faithful. And let us consider how we may spur ________ ____________ on toward love and good deeds, not giving up meeting ______________________ as some are in the habit of doing, but encouraging ________ __________________— and all the more as you see the Day approaching."

I grew up with parents and family who constantly warned, "Don't forsake the gathering of believers." And during my teenage years I'd roll my eyes and wish I could stay home from gathering with fellow believers. But now, in my forties, I see how this warning rings true.

Isolation from the body of Christ can often take us down paths we never thought we'd wander and can leave us susceptible to the lie that we're better off alone. And once we're alone, we're more likely to strive after things that don't lead us to life and life abundantly.

In the garden, after Adam and Eve sinned, what's one of the very first things they did? They hid from God. They hid because, like the prodigal son, they no longer felt worthy of belonging. They no longer felt worthy of their evening walks with the Lord. And when we no longer feel worthy, we often find ourselves striving after things to fill a void that is only designed to be filled by a relationship with our Creator and the community He's called us to.

The goal of this passage in Hebrews isn't to push a legalistic guideline for church attendance. It's an admonishment to belong, to stay connected to the body of Christ, because belonging—truly being known and loved—is for our ultimate good as it's a form of blessing and protection.

When the world today tells you to celebrate your independence, to work hard for your own success, to "do you" without any consideration of others, remember that this is not God's good design. This is the way toward striving and making a name for yourself, but it's also the way to isolation, which ultimately leads us to a place where we are disconnected to the body of Christ and lacking edification and life opportunities for growth and discipleship.

The way to life and life abundantly, according to Scripture, is through belonging to the One who loves you so much that He died for you. You were bought at a price (1 Corinthians 6:20); you are a part of the family of God: one body, many parts. Isolation from that family only leads to despair and heartache. Being part of that family leads to an abundant life. It's what the good father in the parable of the prodigal son represents. The father is welcoming his isolated son back to the abundant life that comes from belonging to a family. He joyfully welcomes his son home and prepares a feast by a warm fire after his son spent months starving until he longed for the pigs' food.

I don't know where this finds you. You might already be practicing the discipline of belonging. But if you aren't, if you've been avoiding belonging for some time, can today be a gentle push to take a step toward belonging? Whether it's calling up that brother or sister in Christ or walking into a new church, let me encourage you to take that next step.

You weren't made to do this alone. Because of Christ, you belong.

Memory Verse

Read your memory verse, Colossians 3:3, and then try to fill in the blanks from memory below.

"________ you ____________, and your ___________ is now ________________ with _____________ in ___________."

Prayer

Reread Proverbs 18:1 (CSB): "One who isolates himself pursues selfish desires; he rebels against all sound wisdom" and spend time asking the LORD to help you fight against the temptation of isolation.

KEY TAKEAWAY: Belonging matters. Being isolated always leads you to a place where you are disconnected from the body of Christ and lacking edification and life-on-life opportunities for growth.

WEEK 4 | **DAY 4**

The Blessing of Belonging

Colossians 4:7–18; 1 Corinthians 12:12–31

I grew up in a small Baptist church in rural Western Kentucky where it wasn't uncommon for me to come home to a table full of various church members. I am forty years old and haven't lived there in over twenty years, and one of our deacons still makes me my favorite homemade ice cream when I'm visiting my parents. Church family expanded beyond Sunday mornings, and many of the families that we worshiped with were the same people I would see at sporting events, holiday celebrations, birthdays, and mundane days in between. One thing about this church; they might not be perfect, but they did a great job of helping people belong.

Not only that, but they made sure that belonging went beyond our local church and community. This rural church supported missionaries all around the world, and it wasn't just financial support where the church wrote a check so they could feel good about themselves. No, they had real relationships with those churches and their leaders. We'd pray for them, they'd visit our church and stay in our homes, and we also knew they were praying for us! It was a mutual friendship.

As a pastor's kid, it was a gift to grow up being prayed for by the body of Christ in Romania, Brazil, and many other countries. And what a gift it was to get to pray over those bodies of believers (and many others) in turn! Just the other day, one of the pastors in Brazil I've known my whole life had open-heart surgery and my parents were giving me updates on how he was recovering. Belonging to one another isn't simply church attendance; it's something deeper than just going through the motions of showing up for a weekly hour-long service.

I am so grateful for this church's faithful example. The church wasn't flashy, and services wouldn't make a great social media post, but this community taught me the meaning of biblical belonging from an early age. I'm forever grateful.

Read Colossians 4:7–18 and answer the questions below.

How many individual people did Paul mention in his sign-off? And how many groups of people does Paul mention?

What does this tell you about these bodies of believers?

Look at Paul's description of his coworkers and list them out below.

Tychicus is a ____________________, a ________________________, and ________________________________.

Onesimus is a _______________ and __________ brother.

Aristarchus, Mark, and Jesus (aka Justus) are _______________ for the kingdom of God and they are a ________________ to Paul.

Epaphras is a prayer warrior who is always _________________ in prayer for the people of Colossians and he is ______________ hard for them.

In looking at these descriptions, how would you describe this fellowship of believers? What stands out to you?

When thinking about belonging to a community like this, wouldn't it be a blessing to be surrounded by people who are similar to the brothers and sisters Paul described in this passage? I read this and immediately started listing my own names and was praising God for the blessing of men and women who have gone before me in the faith.

Think about the community you currently have or have had in the past. List the names of the sisters or brothers in Christ who have blessed your life, and describe them below. While doing so, take a moment to pray over them and ask God to continue to bless their work, their ministries, and their families. (If you don't have anyone who comes to mind, take a moment to write a prayer to God asking Him to help you 1) find a community to belong to, and 2) to be the type of person who is described like Paul described his coworkers.)

Look at verse 16. Who else is this letter for?

It is evident that this letter was written to a body of believers with the intention of its being shared with other churches.

You see, the book of Colossians was written by the apostle Paul to the church at Colossae, but Paul had never met this body of believers before! Epaphras was the one who started this church and had visited Paul in prison. He had told Paul all about their faithfulness, but also about some of their current struggles and societal pressures. Paul had a deep love and concern for his fellow brothers and sisters in Christ that he had never met!

When you belong to the body of Christ, you belong to a local church, but also the global church. You don't just gain local brothers and sisters in Christ; you gain a global community who are partaking in kingdom work together!

The blessing of belonging to the family of God goes beyond proximity or what we have in common.

Look up Galatians 3:28 and fil in the blanks below.

"There is neither ________ nor ______________, neither ______________ nor ______________, nor is there ____________ and ______________, for you are . . . all one in Christ Jesus."

Our proximity, our gender, our ethnicity, our socioeconomic status isn't what makes us belong—it's ____ (hint: the last person mentioned in Gal. 3:28) who makes us one in Him!

There is no amount of striving that earns us a spot in God's family, as we have nothing to prove and nothing to earn, only the name of Christ to proclaim! The blessing of belonging to the family of God is that *all of us* who proclaim Jesus as the Messiah are united and, as we learned in Romans 12, are working together to overcome evil with good.

This is good news, friend. We don't have to walk this road alone. We belong to a body that is united in their love of God and love of others. We get to be loved *and* love other Christians around our communities, our country, and our world!

Read 1 Corinthians 12:12–27 and answer the questions below.

This passage is a lot like what we read on Day 2 of this week in Romans 12. When reading this passage, did you notice any repeated phrases or themes?

Go back through the verses, and every time you see the words "one body," underline them. Every time you see the words "many parts," circle them.

What does this passage say about what it looks like to belong to the body of Christ?

According to these verses, if God has designed His church as one body with many parts, is it wise to live a life of isolation? Why or why not? (Use Scripture as your guide.)

According to verses 22–26, our connectedness is critical to living a healthy life.

Verses 25–26 say that "its parts should have __________ ______________ for each other. If one part suffers, __________ __________ suffers with it; if one part is honored, __________ __________ rejoices with it."

When we talk about belonging and community, we're talking about something greater than church attendance. It's belonging to the family of God that supersedes culture, socioeconomic class, ethnicity, and every other category this world uses to keep us divided. The type of connectedness seen in this passage is radical in our society.

The world tells us that if something doesn't serve you any longer, or causes you discomfort, to just let it go or cut it off. *And yet, this passage says that when one of the members suffers, we ___________________________ (we don't cut them off!).*

The world will tell you that if your coworker or friend gets a promotion and you don't, well, you should work harder and keep hustling until you succeed. *But this passage says that if one of ours is honored, then we should _____________________.*

And what does verse 25 say is the reason for this radical belonging?

Look up the following verses, and list other reasons for biblical community.

Proverbs 27:17

Psalm 133:1–3

Hebrews 10:24–25

In Matthew 22 when Jesus was asked what the greatest commandments were, He told us to love God and love our neighbors as ourselves. Later in Romans 12, we're told what this love should look like practically (we studied this passage on Day 2 of this week).

When I read these passages, I am tempted to start striving and trying to accomplish all of this on my own. The long list of things to do in Romans 12 makes me feel like I need a whole new personality in order to do it! But in 1 Corinthians 12:25, we're told to fight against division in the body, I believe, so we can best accomplish our mission and our kingdom work together!

When you read these passages through the lens of belonging to the body of Christ, remember that Paul's words in Romans (and Colossians) were written to a community of people (one body, many parts); then remember that you have nothing to prove and nothing to earn because Jesus made a way for you to belong. And this kingdom work He has called us to, He's also made a way for us to accomplish—together! Not alone.

This is the blessing of community!

Does knowing you belong to a family bring you relief, anxiety, some other emotion, or a mix of emotions? Explain below.

Take a few moments and write out the ways you are gifted and can contribute to the family of God.

What are some other blessings of belonging to the family of God that we haven't covered in our study?

Memory Verse

Write Colossians 3:3 below, and then speak the words aloud three times, working from memory as best you can. Feel free to use your Bible as needed.

Prayer

Feel free to pray this prayer, or write out your own prayer to God below.

God, thank You for the gift of Your family. Lord, sometimes I don't know quite where I fit in the family of God, and yet I know that belonging matters. Lord, help me find my place in Your family, in Your kingdom. Thank You for Jesus and for His work on the cross so that anyone who proclaims His name can belong in the family of God.

KEY TAKEAWAY: There is no amount of striving that earns us a spot in God's family, as we have nothing to prove and nothing to earn, only the name of Christ to proclaim. This is one of the blessings of belonging to the family of God!

WEEK 4 | **DAY 5**

Reflection and Wrap-Up

Over the last four days we've learned:

- What a gift it is to belong to the family of God (One Body. Many parts!), where our connectedness and shared dependency on Christ ultimately help us overcome evil with good—not just in our own lives, but in our homes, our workplaces, and our communities.
- Belonging matters and being isolated always leads you to a place where you are disconnected from the body of Christ and lacking edification and life on life opportunities for growth.
- There is no amount of striving that earns us a spot in God's family, as we have nothing to prove and nothing to earn, only the name of Christ to proclaim. This is one of the blessings of belonging to the family of God!

Like last week, today is a shorter day. Reread one or all of the passages we read this week and spend some time journaling below by using the provided prompts.

Passages from the week:
Acts 2:42–47 and Romans 12:3–18; Luke 15:11–24 and Ecclesiastes 4:7–12

What is one theme or truth from Scripture that stood out to you the most this week?

Has anything from this week changed, challenged, or shaped your thinking, your actions, or beliefs? If so, how?

What is one idea or verse that has encouraged you that you'd like to carry with you?

In light of what I've learned this week, belonging, to me, means . . .

Finish the sentence: Because of Christ, I . . .

Memory Verse

Write Colossians 3:3 from memory below. (If you can't, no worries! Grace upon grace! Just write it out using your Bible as a reference as needed.)

Prayer

Spend some time talking to God below. Take what you just reflected on and turn it into a prayer. Thank God for what He's shown you this week and ask Him to help you carry it forward.

Key Takeaway: Each day we get to choose to take steps toward belonging or isolation, and whether we know it or not, we're actively choosing one of those two paths. One path leads to destruction and endless striving, and the other leads to belonging to a community of believers. One makes you work harder to survive—like the prodigal son. And one path offers value and meaning as each person has a role to play in the body of Christ and living out the greatest commandments. Which one will you choose?

WEEK FIVE

GRATITUDE vs. GRUMBLING

Key passages for this week: Luke 17:11–19; Philippians 4:1–9 and Colossians 4:3–6; Psalm 107

Introduction

I am not naturally good at gratitude. My heart isn't prone to being thankful in all things.

Perhaps you were hoping to learn from someone adept at gratefulness. Most of what I've learned about gratitude is due to the Lord sanctifying and convicting me over the years. But my prayer is that you'll take what I've learned through my weakness and allow it to strengthen your own muscle of gratitude.

The year I wrote this Bible study was also the year that a lot happened in our family. And when I say a lot, I do mean a lot. I had started the year excited for a "chill year," but a few months in, we had a surprise adoption placement, and the subsequent months were anything but chill. We grew from a family of seven to eight, had multiple floods in our basement and garage, my husband's car was broken into, our HVAC stopped working in the middle of summer, we caught myriad sicknesses that kept us at the pediatrician's office, and the list could go on. Life was life-ing hard, and there were plenty of things that can't be published here, but it was just one of those years.

The Lord provided for us every step of the way, but midway through the year, I was tired and grumbly, constantly looking for the next shoe to drop. And although I was thankful for the good things, the message of the world affirmed my grumbling in the hard things:

"Of course you're tired! You're forty with a newborn and five other kids in tow! It's too much!"

"Of course you're cranky and grumbly! That unexpected hospital bill just came in right after you wrote a check for the HVAC."

"Of course you're short-tempered and impatient. You have every right to be given the amount of times you've had to pivot this year!"

I felt justified in my grumbling. Until the Lord gently, in the middle of another chaotic day, brought to mind 1 Thessalonians 5:15–18:

> *"Make sure that nobody pays back wrong for wrong, but always strive to do what is good for each other and for everyone else.* ***Rejoice always, pray continually, give thanks in all circumstances; for this is God's will for you in Christ Jesus."***

Ouch.

I was definitely not rejoicing and giving thanks in all things. I was praying, but my prayers sounded more like complaining than anything else. And in that moment, something shifted in my heart. I realized that my gratitude muscle was weak, and it needed to be exercised in order for it to grow.

Now, it didn't come naturally and there wasn't a magical moment where my heart was miraculously fixed and gratitude came flowing out. No, real gratitude is gritty; it takes intentionality and a lot of humility, but it's worth fighting for. What I learned in this season was that **the practice of gratitude is a form of protection**. Exercising my gratitude muscles strengthened my resilience, and it fought against the temptation to strive whenever dissatisfaction, jealousy, or fear appeared. Gratitude became my secret weapon, as thankfulness started to shape my perspective and slowly transform my heart and my actions into becoming more like Christ.

By the end of this week, I'm praying you'll start your own gratitude journey. It would be easy to list quick fixes and a 3-step guide to becoming better at gratitude. But just like the previous weeks, this is more about our heart's posture than simply following a guide to fix the symptoms of our problems. But I am praying that you'll walk away from this week with some tools to help exercise and grow that gratitude muscle—because truly, it has made all the difference in living a life free from striving and performance.

WEEK 5 | **DAY 1**

Big Picture Day

Thus far in the study we've learned that as believers who are learning to stop striving, we must choose...

Relationship instead of Religion (Week 1)
Character instead of Charisma (Week 2)
Service instead of Stages (Week 3)
Community instead of Isolation (Week 4)

And this week we'll be learning to choose Gratitude instead of Grumbling (Week 5).

Big Picture Questions

Today is our Big Picture day! Remember that each Day 1 focuses on Scripture. You will simply read and allow the passages to "marinate" before sinking your teeth into the text. Here are three guidelines as you begin each reading:

- Read the Scripture passages for the week in one sitting.
- Highlight any verses, words, or themes that stick out to you.
- In the margins, write any questions you might have as you read.

Consider how the verses relate to each other and to the overall theme of the week.

Read Luke 17:11–19; Philippians 4:1–9 and Colossians 4:3–6; Psalm 107

Now answer each of the questions below:

What does this passage show me about God?

What does this passage show me about this world or humanity?

How does this passage apply to my life? Are there any principles that serve as a guide for the Christian life?

Read Psalm 100:1–5. Spend some time in prayer praising God and thanking Him for His faithfulness. Reflect on this past week, consider ways that God has been faithful, and write them below. Thank God for each.

Memory Verse

Refresh your memorization of Colossians 3:3, and then read this week's memory verse and write it below.

> *"When Christ, who is your life, appears, then you also will appear with him in glory."*
> COLOSSIANS 3:4

Prayer

Feel free to pray this prayer, or write out your own prayer to God below.

God, thank You for Your faithfulness. Thank You that Your love endures forever and that You made us and call us Your own. God, as I look back on this week, this month, and even this past year, I can see how You have gone before me in all things, making a way for Your love and goodness to carry me through the highs, the lows, and the ordinary days in between. Help me to fix my eyes on You. This week, will You transform my heart into one of gratitude? Amen.

WEEK 5 | **DAY 2**

The One Who Said Thanks

Luke 17:11–19

One of my kids is fantastic at spotting an outsider and bringing them into the fold. Another one is an eager cheerleader for others; they're genuinely excited when a sibling gets something. There isn't an ounce of jealousy. And one of our kids, who happens to be a toddler, is naturally good at gratitude. She was born with strong gratitude muscles!

Perhaps it's because she has the most opportunity to say thank you as she's dependent on us for so much. The odd thing is, we never had to teach her to say thank you; she just does it. If one of her siblings gets her a drink, it's "Thank you, sissy!" When I finish doing her hair and getting her ready in the morning, she says, "Thank you, Mama!" When we're at a restaurant, she is the first to say thanks to the wait staff, often prompting the rest of us to flex our gratitude muscles.

Until I saw firsthand how gratitude flowed from her, I don't think I fully understood that some of our personalities naturally come with a stronger affinity toward gratitude. Others of us, well, we have to be more mindful of practicing gratitude. And yet, the Bible is clear, God loves and expects His children to practice the discipline of gratitude.

So, what happens if you're like me and you're not naturally grateful in all things?

The world will tell us that we're just not wired that way and that we have every right to grumble since our world is such a mess. But more often than not, a dissatisfied, grumbly heart turns to striving in search of contentment in places that are always lacking. But God gives us a better way forward. A way that honors Him and is for our good. And like we discussed yesterday, gratitude is our secret weapon against striving for "greener pastures."

Read Luke 17:11–19 and answer the questions below.

Where was Jesus heading?

This is important! Because in the timeline of Jesus' life, this story happens on His journey to the place where He would ultimately face the cross for you and me (hold on to this thought).

Along His journey into the village, who stops Him? What do they say?

During this time period, it was common for people with leprosy to yell out as a warning "Unclean! Unclean!" wherever they went. That way others would know to stay away from them so they would not catch this debilitating disease. These people were social outcasts, pushed aside from society, and left outside the gate of their communities. Jesus would have had every right to simply keep walking away, but He didn't.

The lepers called Him "__________ ______________" (v. 13), and He heard their cries.

Let's chase this rabbit trail for a moment.

On His journey to the cross to offer redemption to those who will receive him, Jesus stopped to care for ten sick outcasts along the way.

This stops me in my tracks every time.

This is our Savior. This is our God.

The God who is calling you to a life of gratitude (as we'll see later in this passage) is the same One who cares about the eternal redemption for *all* who call upon the name of the Lord, while also caring about the physical healing of ten outcasts. He cares about both your future relationship with Him in eternity, while also meeting your needs for today.

Jesus, the great Redeemer, tells the men to go to the priests; and as they went, they were all healed. During that time, in order to be brought back into the community, you had to be declared clean by the local priest.

Look at verses 15–16. What happened next?

What did gratitude look like for the one who returned?

Jesus asked three questions in response to the grateful man's praise. In your own words, summarize His response below.

The question "Where are the other nine?" stands out to me. I've highlighted it in my Bible and written above it, "God doesn't need our gratitude, but it is His will for our lives—see 1 Thessalonians 5:16–18." Let's take a look at that passage.

What are the three commands given in 1 Thessalonians 5:16–18?

Verse 16:

Verse 17:

Verse 18:

In the blanks, write the words that come directly after *each of the commands.*

Rejoice ______________________

Pray _________________________

Give thanks _____ ______ ____________________________.

This means that in every season, your highs, lows, and ordinary days in between should be marked by what?

The end of verse 18 tells us why God is asking this of us. Write it out below:

Why do you believe that it's God's will for us to rejoice always, pray continually, and give thanks in all circumstances?

Let's go back to our passage in Luke. Why do you think the one man came back? Why do you think the other nine did not?

It's easy to be judgmental, but can you imagine?! After years of being ostracized, a priest declares you are clean! Who is the first person you're running to? I know that I'd run straight to my family, tears flowing down my cheeks, ready to feel the warmth of their embraces. I would probably only think about going back and saying thank you when my head hit my pillow that night. After all, for some of us, that gratitude muscle is weaker than others.

How does Scripture describe the one who came back in verses 16 and 18?

"He threw himself at Jesus' feet and thanked him—and he was a ________________."

"Has no one returned to give praise to God except this ________________________?"

Why do you think that's an important detail to note?

I believe the underlying answer to that question is seen in Jesus' response. Jesus was between Samaria and Galilee, so it is likely that area was populated by gentiles and Jews alike. Jesus makes note that it's not the Jewish ones, the religious ones, who come back to express gratitude to God for their healing; it's a foreigner.

And yet, verse 19 says that this foreigner's _________________________ is the thing that made him well.

His faith was stronger than the faith of the nine religious men!

One commentary explains:

> We're supposed to recognize the irony here: It's the Samaritan foreigner who returns with thanks—not the nine Jewish people. God's people take him for granted and don't even give thanks, but this man outside the covenant of Israel recognizes what has happened and falls down in worship.
>
> Here's another reason I love Jesus: almost no one reading this would even hope to know God if the Lord had not determined, before the world was

created, to establish Israel as his chosen people but then send the Messiah to justify Gentiles as well (Gal. 3:8).[19]

As a gentile, grafted into the family of God (unless you're Jewish!), do you identify more with the Samaritan who was quick to express gratitude? Or do you identify with the religious Jews, who, as the commentary states, often took God's provision for granted?

Sister, like I've said throughout this study, I'm not here to shame you. You might have a strong gratitude muscle and you're able to look at your life and be acutely aware of the many blessings you have. Or you might look around at the rubble and wonder, "How in the world am I supposed to find something to be grateful for in this mess?" Or maybe you are a person who too often looks at the green pastures of a friend or acquaintance's life and you're having a hard time being grateful for what the Lord has given you.

I don't know where life finds you, but in all of these scenarios God is there, protecting and working all things for our good. And because of that, we practice what Scripture asks of us: **On our best days, we thank God because every good and perfect gift comes from above.[20] And on our worst days, we thank God because we know that in all things He is working for our good and His glory, and one day He'll right every wrong.[21]**

Growing in gratitude is not something to cross off your list of being a good Christian. No, it's the key to a life free from striving after a different set of circumstances. It's your road map to suffering well and choosing contentment. It's critical to living a joyful life in seasons of comfort because you rightly understand that all of your days are held in the hands of a good and faithful Father.

---

19. Thabiti Anyabwile, *Christ-Centered Exposition: Exalting Jesus in Luke* (B&H Publishing, 2018), 259.
20. James 1:17.
21. Romans 8:28; Revelation 21:1–7.

Memory Verse

Read Colossians 3:4, and then try your best to fill in the blanks from memory below (but remember, it's okay if you need to look back at Scripture!).

"When Christ, who is ________ ________, appears, then you also will ___________ with him _____ __________."

Prayer

What are some things you can thank God for today? Read the verse below and write out things you can be thankful for and pray a prayer of gratitude for the ways He has provided. Remember, there is nothing too big or small for this list. It can be something as simple as the weather, the kindness of a stranger or friend, or being able to pay your rent this month.

KEY TAKEAWAY: Gratitude is not rote obedience. It's not another thing to check off a list for how to live a good Christian life; it's your secret weapon against striving for places and things that God has not called you to.

Choosing Gratitude

Colossians 4:2–6; Philippians 4:4–9

Have you ever heard of the phrase "fake it till you make it"?

I've heard this used as an encouragement to someone with imposter syndrome, fearing they don't fit in at a new job. I've heard it said in a coaching conversation about sales. But one space I never want to hear that phrase is in the context of Christian community and our faith practices.

Here's why.

The passages we're studying today are going to give us direct commandments on how to live our lives, but the truth is, sometimes we just don't feel like it. There are days when I don't feel like being prayerful. There are days and even weeks that go by when I don't choose to think and speak what is true and right. And, quite frankly, there are seasons when I actually *want* to be grumbly instead of choosing to be grateful and thinking on heavenly things!

The answer to this heart issue is **not** to just "fake it till you make it."

No, the answer is to choose to obey God's Word even when our hearts don't feel like it. And although this might appear to be similar on the outside, it's actually quite different internally because we are honest about the nature of our heart! You see, we don't do this by pretending to be something that we're not. Instead, we acknowledge the gap between where our hearts currently are and where we want them to be (and most importantly where He wants them to be!). Then we honor our truest identity, being a daughter of God, and we choose obedience and submission to the Father's way of living instead of clinging to our own while using our feelings as excuses.

That's not faking it. That's not pretense.

It's honestly assessing that our hearts are not where we want them to be. And instead of pretending that gap doesn't exist, we trust that God's ways are better than ours and that obeying Him will lead us to our ultimate good. The gap slowly closes by obeying His commands and following His ways.

We're not faking it until we make it because we're not faking it at all!

Today, we're going to look at what God is asking us to do, all the while being mindful of the gap.

Read Colossians 4:2–6 and answer the questions below.

The very first word in the first verse is an imperative verb, meaning this isn't a suggestion. Paul isn't softening it and saying, "When you have the time, would you mind . . . " Instead, the first word is a command.

Underline that word in your Bible and write it below.

In your own words, define the word you wrote above.

That feels like a pretty strong word, doesn't it? It makes me think of an Olympic athlete who has put time and effort into chasing one specific goal through early morning practices, a focus on their nutrition and water intake, and an early bedtime so they can get enough sleep. They are focused on a goal, devoted to it, if you will—and their actions show it.

What would it look like for you to be a person who is devoted to prayer? (Hint: There is no right or wrong answer here. This question is just a catalyst for you to examine your heart and life.)

According to verse 2, what are the two characteristics that should describe our approach to prayer?

1.

2.

What do you think it means to be watchful?

I love how the Christian Standard Bible states Colossians 4:2. It says, "Devote yourselves to prayer; ***stay alert in it*** with thanksgiving."

Be watchful, and stay alert in your prayer with thanksgiving. In other words, thanksgiving helps us be watchful in prayer; it helps us to be mindful in our current circumstances.

Again, gratitude isn't just the act of being thankful; it is our secret weapon to living a life of having nothing to prove and nothing to earn as gratitude helps us to be prayerfully dependent on a good and faithful Father rather than dependent on ourselves. When we are praying prayers of thanksgiving to God about our daily lives, we fight against the enemy's messaging that what we have isn't enough, that we have something more to prove, or that our lives are too messy or too broken. God has designed this world and our hearts to be wired in such a way that gratitude is for our ultimate good and it's through gratitude that we find freedom from worrying, from striving, and from longing for places and things God hasn't called us to.

Read Colossians 4:3–4. What else is Paul asking them to pray for?

For the modern-day reader, what is one takeaway for your own prayer life?

Look at verses 5–6. We have more imperative verbs in these verses. (Honestly, I love a good direct command. It's easier for my heart to get on board when I know exactly what's being asked of me.) What are the commands given to us in these verses?

How do these commands connect to the initial request to be devoted in prayer, being watchful and thankful?

Read Philippians 4:4–7 and answer the questions below.

We have more imperative commands. Again, even when our hearts might not feel like it, Scripture is providing a road map for closing the gap between where our hearts currently are, and where we want them to be (more like Jesus' heart).

In verses 4–7, what commands are similar to the ones we read in the previous passage in Colossians?

What commands are new? List them below.

In verse 4, we see Paul repeating himself. In my home, when one of us repeats ourselves, it usually means that we're trying to communicate something important.

Look up the passages below. Why do you think the command to rejoice is important?

1 Thessalonians 5:16–18

Psalm 103:1–5

Proverbs 17:22

1 Peter 1:8–9

In verses 4–6, there are phrases that give context or additional meaning to the passage. Below, fill in the blanks with the missing phrases.

"Rejoice in the Lord ____________________. I will say it again: Rejoice! Let your gentleness be evident to _____. The Lord is near. Do not be anxious about anything, _____ ____ ________________________, by prayer and petition, with thanksgiving, present your requests to God. And the peace of God _______ __________________ _____ ____________________, will guard your hearts and your minds in Christ Jesus."

Circle that word "always."

I don't *always* feel like rejoicing. It's hard to rejoice when your life feels like it's in shambles. It can feel hard to rejoice even when you're just experiencing minor inconveniences from living in a broken world.

The passage also says that our gentleness should be evident to ______.

Are you noticing a pattern yet in this passage? Paul is hitting home that this way of living is not reserved just for the moments we deem appropriate, but they're for all of our days—the highs, lows, and ordinary moments in between.

Let's look again at Philippians 4:6 and Colossians 4:2. In both verses we see a connection between prayer and gratitude. Why do you think Paul keeps putting these two things together?

Notice the command that you wrote above from verse 6. We're told to not be anxious in anything, but in every situation *(circle it), with prayer and thanksgiving, we bring our requests to God. Do you find it hard or easy to not be anxious in difficult situations?*

Let's recap the circumstances that Paul is asking us to be obedient in.

In verse 4, we're told to rejoice ______________________________.

In verse 5, we're told to be gentle, or reasonable, to __________.

In verse 6, we're told that in ________________________ we should through prayer and thanksgiving bring our requests to God.

This is countercultural!

When we open our phones or watch the news, what we see modeled before us is a world that constantly grumbles at its own brokenness. If someone wrongs us, by the world's standards, we have every right to retaliate. If suffering hits, it's considered naïve to choose gratitude and see God's hand in all things. And we are driven by fear with every news cycle and article written.

These direct commandments from Scripture are asking us to live a better way; but make no mistake, **it's radical living.**

In verse 7, we're given sturdy ground to stand on and a "why" for our radical living. What is this sturdy ground?

And remember that phrase that you wrote above: "which transcends all understanding."

This peace doesn't make sense by the world's standards, but in the kingdom of God, it transcends all and has the power to guard your______________________ and your______________________ in Christ Jesus.

When there is a gap between where are hearts currently are and where we want them to be, this peace from God protects our hearts and minds and is the way we close that gap.

Read Philippians 4:8–9 and answer the questions below.

If we want to live lives free of grumbling, with nothing to prove and nothing to earn, prayer and gratitude and rejoicing in *all things* is the way forward. But maybe you're like me, and you're still wondering how to actually practice this without "faking it."

Verses 8–9 give us our answer. Using the passage, write out what we should be training our brains to think about.

Look up the passages below and answer the question: How do we train our brains to think on those things listed in Philippians 4?

2 Corinthians 10:5

Romans 12:1–2

It's normal for your "want to" to be broken. It's normal to not want to rejoice always, to not want to be grateful in all things, and to not want to be prayerful in every situation.

This is part of being human.

If I waited to brush my teeth until I felt like it, I would probably only do it twice a week (ew, gross, I know), and as a result, my teeth would rot and fall out. Feelings are helpful. They're important to notice, but they don't drive our decisions. And yet, **instead of faking it until we make it, we acknowledge our limited humanity and trust in God's sovereign design**.

I know, we don't usually have application points in the middle of the week. But I don't want you to miss this. This week, when your heart wants to grumble, I want you to grab hold of that thought, and then immediately take it to God and pray about it with gratitude. We can choose to follow the road map provided by Paul in Philippians and Colossians because we know that it's for our ultimate good.

I've created a "What's good?!" space below for you to keep track of the things you're grateful for, or you can create a "What's good?!" note on your phone.

What's Good?!

Memory Verse

Read Colossians 3:4, and then try to fill in the blanks from memory below.

"When Christ, who is ________ ________, appears, then you also will __________ with him _____ __________."

Prayer

Spend some time praying and asking God to reveal the gap between where your heart is actually and where He wants it to be. Use 2 Corinthians 10:5 as your guide and write out your prayer or use this prayer below.

Father, Your holy Word says that we have the power, through Christ, to take every thought captive and make it obedient to You. Lord, some days I don't know how to do that. Please help me take every thought captive and bring it to You. Lord, when I start to grumble, may Your Spirit prompt me to bring my heartaches and complaints to You and to choose gratitude instead. Create in me a clean heart, oh, God! One that exudes gratefulness for my salvation and Your redemption. Thank You, God, for saving me, for redeeming me, and for not leaving me just as I am. I love You, Jesus. Amen.

KEY TAKEAWAY: Choosing gratitude in a world that encourages grumbling isn't faking it. It's just like brushing your teeth; it's choosing to do what's best for your soul in the long run even when you don't feel like it.

WEEK 5 | **DAY 4**

Let the Redeemed of the Lord Say So

Psalm 107

The last two days we've learned that gratitude is our secret weapon to a life with nothing to prove and nothing to earn, and that choosing gratitude when we don't feel like it isn't faking it. Instead, it's choosing to trust that God's way of living is better than the one this world has to offer.

Today, we're going to put what we've learned into practice. We're going to spend time looking at the book of Psalms and our own lives. Our study will include a guided time of thankfulness after a brief inductive study.

After all, what good is gaining knowledge about these choices without taking the time for our hearts to learn how to put them into practice?

Read Psalm 107 and answer the prompts below.

While reading, every time you notice a reference to thankfulness or gratitude, circle the phrases.

Look at verse 1. Starting right off the bat, we're given another imperative. What are we commanded to do and why?

Verse 2 says, "Let the ____________________ of the Lord tell their ______________ . . ." As a person who is redeemed, does telling your story of redemption feel natural or difficult? Why?

Let's take a look the four "Somes" listed in Psalm 107. In the quadrants below, write out how Scripture describes these people.

SOME #1: Those who wandered in wastelands (vv. 4–9)	**SOME #2: Those who sat in darkness (vv. 10–16)**
Ex. They were discontent, not able to settle anywhere (v. 4)	
SOME #3: Those who were foolish and rebellious (vv. 17–22)	**SOME #4: Those who were journeyers (vv. 23–32)**

Personally, I identify with Some #4. I grew up in a Christian home, and so I don't have a wild testimony, but it's still powerful nonetheless! Because whenever God redeems a wayward heart, it's a miracle. And along my journey of life, I've seen God move in miraculous ways. I've walked through trials and had my heart crushed into pieces from the weight of sin in this world, and God heard my cries and brought me out of my distress (v. 28). But enough about me, what about you?

Out of the four types of people redeemed, which one do you identify with and why?

Did you notice any repeated phrases or verses in this chapter? (If you need a hint, there is a verse in all of the "Somes" sections that is the same.) Write out the verse below.

Notice, in all four different examples provided, the same call to thankfulness is there! Why do you think that is?

The same call to thankfulness exists because everyone who has been redeemed by the Lord has the same reason to give thanks. Though our experiences and circumstances may vary, God's unfailing love does *not*. It's always the same. It never changes. His salvation and redemption for all of mankind is *free* and worthy of our gratitude! Amen?

Let's take a look at God's unfailing love described in Psalm 107. In the quadrants below, write out how Scripture describes how God redeemed these people:

God's redemption for SOME #1: Those who wandered in wastelands (vv. 4–9)	God's redemption for SOME #2: Those who sat in darkness (vv. 10–16)
Ex. He delivered them from their distress and led them to a straight path to a place where they could settle.	
God's redemption for SOME #3: Those who were foolish and rebellious (vv. 17–22)	**God's redemption for SOME #4: Those who were journeyers (vv. 23–32)**

Look at verse 43. It says, "Let the one who is wise ______________ these things and ______________________ the loving deeds of the Lord."

I don't know about you, but I want to be wise. So, let's take a moment to reflect on these things and remember the ways the Lord has been loving toward us. Looking back on your life, how has God redeemed you—not just your moment of salvation (although *this* is most important and should be included)? But how has He delivered you and shown His unfailing love for you throughout your life?

For example, if this were my personal Bible study, I'd get real and not be superficial. I'd list how God saved me at a young age but also guided me and never left me my whole life. I'd list how a few years into my marriage, I thought it was falling apart and there was no way to fix it. We were headed straight toward divorce, but God redeemed it and restored it. I'd write about how my girls were born far too early, and how those days in the NICU were terrifying, but God was with us every step of the way. I'd write about how God ordained adoption to be a part of our family story, and how I've witnessed Him show up not just for our kids, but for their first families as well. I'd write about the first time I witnessed a woman place a baby she had just birthed into my arms, and how she chose a good and safe life for that child while sacrificing her own body, and how watching her leave the hospital with empty arms changed me and broke me in ways I never expected. But God stepped in and redeemed—and is still redeeming—many of the hearts broken from that day. And so, I want you to share openly too! We all have a story to tell, and as Psalm 107:2 says, "Let the redeemed of the Lord tell their story."

How has God redeemed you?

Read the following passages and list what we're called to do and the reason for doing it. (Hint: For the reason, look for words like "for the Lord," etc.)

Psalm 136:1–26

Psalm 95:1–5

Psalm 100:1–5

Now, with those verses in mind, practice what we've been commanded to do. We're going to exercise those gratitude muscles! In the space below, give thanks to the Lord.

Write out a prayer of gratitude for the things you wrote about above. Again, make it personal. You can start general, but allow for the Lord to bring specific instances to mind when He's shown you His unfailing love. Start praising and thanking Him below.

When I was writing out all the many ways God has shown His unfailing love for me, more often than not, hardship and heartache also came to mind. Most of the situations I listed weren't of my own choosing, but from living in a broken world. And here's where the practice of gratitude becomes key to becoming the person God has called us to be.

Where Satan sees opportunity to break us and the world sees opportunity to encourage us to grumble or strive for a different set of circumstances, these are our very own battlegrounds for gratitude! Because this is where our God shows up and shows out every time.

Scripture tells us that for those who are in Christ Jesus, God will work *all things* for our good (Romans 8:28). We see that He is a good God who binds up the brokenhearted and turns sorrow into joy (Isaiah 61). And so, we can be grateful in *all things*, because gratitude can lead you to a place of true contentment in any and every situation. Exercising that muscle of gratitude will only lead to our good and His glory.

Again, this week when you start to grumble, let me encourage you to keep taking it to the Father. Do it for the big things and the small things. God is delighted when His children come to Him with their burdens and their praise!

Memory Verse

Write Colossians 3:4 below, and then speak the words aloud three times, working from memory as best you can. Feel free to use your Bible as needed.

Prayer

We already spent time in prayer above, but I want to leave you with this brief prayer to pray this week whenever you find yourself starting to grumble.

Lord, I'm coming to You grumbly again. I am releasing my own control over ___________ ______________________________________, and I am thanking You for being a God who is good in all things and whose love for me endures forever. I don't understand what is happening, but I do understand that in all things, I have reason for thanks. Thank You for Your salvation. Thank You for being a God who redeems. Thank You for Your unfailing love. Thank You for never leaving me or forsaking me. Thank You for Your provision. God, I'm asking for eyes to see Your goodness in this. In Jesus' name, amen.

KEY TAKEAWAY: "Give thanks to the LORD, for He is good; His love endures forever." (Psalm 136:1)

Reflection and Wrap-Up

Over the last four days we've learned:

- Gratitude is not rote obedience. It's not another thing to check off a list for how to live a good Christian life; it's your secret weapon against striving for places and things that God has not called you to.
- Choosing gratitude in a world that encourages grumbling isn't faking it. It's just like brushing your teeth; it's choosing to do what's best for your soul in the long run even when you don't feel like it.
- Give thanks to the Lord, for He is good; His love endures forever. (Psalm 136:1)

Like last week, today is a shorter day. Reread one or all of the passages we read this week and spend some time journaling below by using the provided prompts.

Passages from the week:
Luke 17:11–19; Philippians 4:1–9 and Colossians 4:3–6; Psalm 107

What is one theme or truth from Scripture that stood out to you the most this week?

Has anything from this week changed, challenged, or shaped your thinking, your actions, or beliefs? If so, how?

What is one idea or verse that has encouraged you that you'd like to carry with you?

In light of what I've learned this week, choosing gratitude over grumbling looks like . . .

Finish the sentence: Because of Christ, I . . .

Memory Verse

Write Colossians 3:4 from memory below. If you can't, no worries! Grace upon grace! Write it out using your Bible as a reference.

Prayer

Spend some time talking to God below. Take what you just reflected on and turn it into a prayer, and write it out below. Thank God for what He's shown you this week, and ask Him to help you carry it forward.

KEY TAKEAWAY: Each day, we're given many opportunities to choose gratitude or grumbling. But for those who are redeemed, one way we live radically is to choose gratitude even when we don't feel like. This isn't rote obedience or faking it; rather it's the road map to a life of resilience and contentment, with nothing to prove and nothing to earn.

WEEK SIX

ROOTED vs. RESTLESS

Key Passages for the week: Colossians 2: 4–23; Ephesians 3:14–4:6; Ephesians 4:14–32

Introduction

According to the American Psychological Association, more than half of the adults in the United States report that they are very restless.[22] I'm not surprised by that at all. I look around at my peers and see many who aren't satisfied with the status quo in their lives. The job they once prayed for is now underwhelming, the family they once longed for is stressing them out, and the church they eagerly joined turns out to be full of sinful humans.

I get it. I'm not casting stones.

It's tempting to look left or right and be dissatisfied because we all live in a broken world, full of broken people. And with more resources at our fingertips, it's easy to believe that if we just had a new job or a new family or a new church or a new season, our life would be so much better.

So, we work harder for that promotion, or we keep starting over at a new job. We church hop until we find the church that best fits our preferences, at least until that one disappoints us, and we move on to the next. We ghost our friends and family when they start to get on our nerves, and with the world at our fingertips, we either isolate and use technology as a substitute for friendship, or we find a new friend group.

---

22. American Psychological Association (2020). *Stress in America™ 2020: A National Mental Health Crisis.* https://www.apa.org/news/press/releases/stress/2020/sia-mental-health-crisis.pdf.

Does any of this sound familiar? It might not describe you exactly, but it is a general description of many in our society. Because this is the advice that the world gives. Being restless and dissatisfied with your life is a key component to the world keeping you chasing (and often purchasing) the next new thing. And wow! Just reading all of that makes me tired. It's a whole lot of striving for temporary satisfaction only to grow dissatisfied again with time.

And yet, as we'll learn this week, we get to choose how we live, and the good news of Jesus offers a better way forward. You see, the way of Jesus isn't to be tossed to and fro by every new ideology the world throws at us. The way of Jesus isn't to chase after every shiny new thing that captures our attention. **The way of Jesus is to live on mission, being rooted and built up in Him (Colossians 2:7).**

This is what I want for us.

I want to see a generation of women who are so deeply rooted in Christ that they're not captured by the materialism that is so accessible on those tiny devices we carry in our pockets.

I long to see a generation of women who don't care what the world says about their body composition or how many wrinkles they have; they know their worth because they're rooted and grounded in Christ.

I want to see a generation of women who know that they are beloved daughters of a King and that changes the way they carry themselves into every room they walk in to.

I pray for women who don't bloom where they're planted because they read it on a coffee mug, but they stay in the trenches and show up in hard spaces because they understand their unique role to play in the kingdom.

I long for a generation of women who are rooted instead of restless, because as we read in Romans 12:21, rooted women are not overcome by evil, but they overcome evil with good.

And, sister, this isn't just a pipe dream. This can be me. This can be you. This is who we were meant to be, together.

Lord, let it be so.

WEEK 6 | DAY 1

Big Picture Day

Thus far in the study we've learned that as believers who are learning to stop striving, we must choose...

Relationship instead of Religion (Week 1)
Character instead of Charisma (Week 2)
Service instead of Stages (Week 3)
Community instead of Isolation (Week 4)
Gratitude instead of Grumbling (Week 5)

And this week we'll be learning to choose Rooted instead of Restless (Week 6).

Big Picture Questions

Today is our Big Picture day! Remember that each Day 1 focuses on Scripture. You will simply read and allow the passages to "marinate" before sinking your teeth into the text. Here are three guidelines as you begin each reading:

- Read the Scripture passages for the week in one sitting.
- Highlight any verses, words, or themes that stick out to you.
- In the margins, write any questions you might have as you read.

Consider how the verses relate to each other and to the overall theme of the week.

Read Colossians 2:4–23; Ephesians 3:14–4:6; Ephesians 4:14–32

Now answer each of the questions below:

What does this passage show me about God?

What does this passage show me about this world or humanity?

How does this passage apply to my life? Are there any principles that serve as a guide for the Christian life?

Read Proverbs 19:23: "The fear of the LORD leads to life; then one rests content, untouched by trouble." Spend some time reflecting on that proverb. What would "content, untouched by trouble" look like in your life?

Memory Verse

Yay! We made it! This week we'll be putting them all together.

> *"Since, then, you have been raised with Christ, set your hearts on things above, where Christ is, seated at the right hand of God. Set your minds on things above, not on earthly things. For you died, and your life is now hidden with Christ in God. When Christ, who is your life, appears, then you also will appear with him in glory."*
> Colossians 3:1–4

Prayer

Feel free to pray this prayer, or write out your own prayer to God below.

God, this week as I study Your Word, will You open my eyes to ways I'm restless? More than anything, I want to be rooted in You and You alone. God, give me wisdom to see the areas of my life that need to be rooted in Your ways instead of the world's. Your ways are better; help me believe this and live this out. In Jesus' name. Amen.

WEEK 6 | DAY 2

In Christ Alone

Colossians 2:4–23

Have you ever heard the popular phrase, "There is nothing new under the sun"? It's from a verse that says, "What has been will be again, what has been done will be done again; there is nothing new under the sun" (Ecc. 1:9). When I read the passage for today, this verse immediately came to my mind.

In today's passage, Paul is talking to a church in Colossae about being rooted in Christ and what that looks like. But he's also warning against a type of Gnosticism that, while it sounded morally good, was based in ancient human tradition instead of being rooted in the good news of Jesus. In fact, many of the people who were trying to lure away these believers were considered to have great moral standing in their community![23]

Sound familiar? You can login to a number of social media apps and quickly be inundated with some "good" advice and wisdom from ancient human tradition, *but* much of it tickles our ears and offers false hope in the false gods of idolatry, materialism, and moralistic therapeutic deism.

Moralistic therapeutic deism is prevalent on social media today. It's the idea that a god exists and created everything, but he's not really involved or in control of our day-to-day activities. The goal is to be a good human, be happy, and be fair with one another. And at the end of our lives, good people go to heaven.

So much of this "be happy and be a good person" ideology shapes what we consume. That doesn't sound so bad, does it? And yet, it is a message that isn't rooted in the

23. R. Kent Hughes, *Philippians, Colossians, and Philemon: The Fellowship of the Gospel and the Supremacy of Christ* (Crossway, 2013), 274–75.

life-changing work of the gospel. Today we're going to wrestle with this passage from Colossians and gain wisdom that will help us stay rooted and built up in Christ, not in deceptive philosophies.

Read Colossians 2:4–15 and answer the questions below.

Why is Paul writing this portion of the letter according to verses 4–5?

In verse 6, there is a qualifier for the instructions Paul is about to give. Who are the people these instructions are for?

This qualifier is important because this way of living isn't for those who merely like to dabble in Jesus; it's for people who have been changed by receiving the gift of the Messiah, so much so that they live their lives in Him.

This qualifier is also a good standard to go by when we're gleaning wisdom from others. Are the voices you're consuming mostly from people who follow a "be happy and be a good person" ideology? Or are you listening to people who are continuing to walk with Jesus?

Spend some time thinking about the media you consume, and list the voices below that you want to invest more time in.

I love how both the NIV and CSB translate verses 6–7. Let's look at them side by side and notice their subtle differences.

> *So then, just as you received Christ Jesus as Lord, continue to live your lives in him, rooted and built up in him, strengthened in the faith as you were taught, and overflowing with thankfulness.*
> COLOSSIANS 2:6–7 (NIV)

> *So then, just as you have received Christ Jesus as Lord, continue to walk in him, being rooted and built up in him and established in the faith, just as you were taught, and overflowing with gratitude.*
> COLOSSIANS 2:6–7 (CSB)

Sometimes, it's helpful to look at various translations when you wonder what exactly something means. For example, when I read this passage in the NIV I asked, "What does it mean to live my life in Him?" And I think the CSB explains it well: Keep walking in Him. Keep taking your next steps in line with the ways of Jesus.

In verses 6–7, there are four characteristics of a person who has received Christ Jesus. What are they? Feel free to use the NIV or CSB or a mix of the two to answer this.

Based on those four things above, what would it look like in your life to live out these four characteristics? In the chart on the next page, take a moment to pray, and then list practical ways you can walk in Him, be rooted and built up in Him, be strengthened in the faith, and be overflowing with gratitude.

What is the warning we find in Colossians 2:8?

According to verse 8, how are these worldly philosophies described?

Verses 9–15 serve as a reminder of who we are and whose we are! In the space below rewrite these verses in your own words, reminding yourself who exactly your Messiah is.

Read Colossians 2:16–24 and answer the questions below.

There are multiple "Do Nots" in verses 16–21. List them below.

Colossians 2:16

Colossians 2:18

In Col. 2:20-21, what are some of the man-made rules people were telling the Colossians they should be following?

Some of these commands might sound odd to you, but remember Paul was writing to a specific audience. The church of Colossae was currently feeling societal pressure to practice a philosophy that combined some practices of Judaism with Greek Gnosticism. This is considered the practice of syncretism, a combination of two belief systems or religions.

You see, there were rites and rituals that were familiar to their faith, but the danger was that additional practices were added with just enough of the truth that it was enticing. One commentator said that this philosophy "was presented as 'something more' that would elevate the ignorant Colossian Christians from their crude baby-faith to the truly deeps things of God."[24] **But the gospel stands alone. It doesn't need anything added to it!**

I've heard many preachers say it this way:

> Jesus + Anything Else = Nothing
> Jesus + Other Beliefs and Spiritual Practices (Syncretism) = Nothing
> But . . . Jesus + Nothing = Everything! (This is the gospel!)

Verse 20 summarizes this well: "Since you died ________________ to the elemental spiritual forces of this world, why, as though you still belonged to the world, do you submit to its rules?"

In other words, Jesus is sufficient! The Messiah is the only one who saves.

The message of the world is:

> Jesus + Being a good person
> Jesus + Having a large bank account
> Jesus + Living a happy life

This is syncretism. This is moralistic therapeutic deism. This is not the gospel. The message of the gospel is that we are saved by grace through faith in Christ alone (Eph. 2:8–9). And yet, I too fall prey to the messages of this world. There are many times I still try to take on the role of Christ and add something to His work, such as:

24. R. Kent Hughes, *Philippians, Colossians, and Philemon: The Fellowship of the Gospel and the Supremacy of Christ* (Crossway, 2013), 272–73.

Jesus + Making sure I'm being a good wife/mom/friend/daughter/neighbor
Jesus + Making sure I'm raising good kids
Jesus + Making sure I'm successful in my career

These aren't bad things in and of themselves, yet sometimes I work on these as if my salvation depends on it. And that just isn't the case! Those are my "Jesus+" temptations, but what about you?

What ways are you tempted to add to the work of Jesus?

Jesus +

Jesus +

Jesus +

Friends, the Jesus+*anything* combination is one that always leads to more striving and ultimately a restless and dissatisfied spirit. But the book of Colossians reminds us that Christ alone is above all things, and He alone holds all things together (Colossians 1:17).

Look back at the first word in Col. 2:16. Circle the word "Therefore" and write "Because of this." Draw an arrow to the previous verses.

- Because we received Christ Jesus as Lord and are continuing to walk in Him (v. 6) . . .
- Because we are rooted and built up in Him (v. 7) . . .
- Because we do not want to be taken captive by any deceptive philosophies (v. 8) . . .
- Because Christ bought us, saved us, and redeemed us (vv. 9–15) . . .
- Because we've been buried with Christ and raised in Him through our faith (v. 12) . . .

***Therefore,* we do not live by the world's rules and philosophies, but we live in Christ.**

Verse 17 describes the world's philosophies perfectly by stating that they "are a ________________________ of things that were to come; the reality, however, is found in ___________________."

Let's look at v. 23 in the CSB:

> *"Although these have a reputation for wisdom by promoting self-made religion, false humility, and severe treatment of the body, they are not of any value in curbing self-indulgence."* Colossians 2:23 (CSB)

What does this verse tell us about the world's rules and philosophies?

This world will keep you striving and restless by trying to add to what Jesus has already done. And yet, the good news of Jesus is that He alone saves. He alone is holding all things together. And He alone is reconciling all things in heaven and on earth.

Memory Verse

Read Colossians 3:1–4, *and then try your best to fill in the blanks from memory below (but remember, it's okay if you need to look back at Scripture!).*

"Since, then, you have been ________________ with ________________, set your ______________ on things above, where ________________ is, seated at the _____________ ____________ of God. _______ your ________________ on things above, not on ________________things. For you ______________, and your _________ is now hidden with ________________ in God. When Christ, who is your _________ appears, then you also will _______________ with him in glory."

Prayer

God thank You that because of Jesus, I don't have to strive to find my identity in any other worldly possession or position. Lord, would You help me to live a life rooted in You and You alone? Guard my heart and mind against worldly philosophies that might draw me away from You. Help me to remember each day that the gospel of Jesus stands alone and that I don't have to add anything to it. Thank You for Your great love for me. In Jesus' name.

KEY TAKEAWAY: The philosophies of this world will keep you striving and restless by adding to the work of Jesus. And yet, the good news of Jesus is that He alone saves. He alone is holding all things together. And He alone is reconciling all things in heaven and on earth. So instead of striving, we choose to be rooted and built up in Christ and Christ alone.

Rooted in Love

Ephesians 3:14–4:6

Today, we're in another letter from Paul. One of the things I love about the epistles is that when we read them as a whole, we can pick up on similar themes and ideals that Paul was teaching the early churches. At this point in the study, you've read the entire book of Colossians. (Surprise! You finished it yesterday.) And today, you'll see that some of the language and concepts that Paul used in his letter to the church of Colossae, he also used in his letter to the Ephesians.

The section of Ephesians we're reading today is divided into two parts. Ephesians 3:14–21 is a prayer from Paul for the Ephesian church. Two things to remember: 1) This prayer isn't for an individual, but for a body of believers, so 2) even though you might be doing this Bible study as an individual, remember you are a part of this global church, meaning, this prayer applies to *you*!

And the second part that we're reading, Ephesians 4:1–6, begins a section of the letter where Paul is instructing these believers on what it looks like to live out the Christian faith in the context of community. We'll get into more of that in Day 4, but we will stick our toes in the water today as we continue this journey of learning what it looks like to be rooted instead of restless.

Read Ephesians 3:14–21 and answer the questions below.

Paul says "for this reason I kneel" in verse 14. What is the reason he's kneeling and praying?

Paul's prayer is a brief one, but it mentions God the Father, God the Son, and God the Spirit many times. How many times does Paul mention God in these eight verses?

What do verses 16–17 say the role of God is in our lives?

(Verse 16) Out of His riches, God may ______________________________ us with power through His Spirit in our ___________________________.

(Verse 17) Christ may ___________________ in our hearts through faith.

According to verses 17–19, what is our role in light of belonging to the family of God?

(Verse 17) We are to be ________________________ and __________________________ in love.

(Verse 18) We have power, together with as God's holy people to _________________ the vastness of the _____________ of Christ.

(Verse 19) We are to know this _____________ that surpasses understanding, and be ______________________ with the fullness of God.

With so much emphasis on God's work in our lives in Paul's prayer, it is freeing to know that apart from Christ dwelling in our hearts through faith (v. 17), we cannot accomplish the rest of what this passage is asking us to do. Again, the Christian life isn't about mere behavior modification. It's about believing that Christ alone can save us and allowing Him to strengthen us so that we can then live lives worthy of our callings! As our hearts are changed, our behavior starts to follow suit.

Do you notice any phrases that are similar to one of the ones we focused on yesterday in Colossians? (Hint: Look at the end of verse 17, and if you need another hint, flip back to Colossians 2:7.) Underline that phrase and write it below.

Is there another word or phrase that has been repeated in this passage today? (Hint: Look at Ephesians 3:17–19 and Colossians 4:2.)

Read Ephesians 1:3–10. This is the first time the word above was used in Paul's letter. Fill in the missing phrase in vv. 4–5:

"For he chose us in him before the creation of the world to be holy and blameless in his sight. ____ _________ he predestined us for adoption to sonship through Jesus Christ, in accordance with his pleasure and will."

According to these verses, what does the phrase "in love" mean for us?

With that in mind, what do you think it means to be rooted and established in love? (Write it down below . . . and hold that thought because Paul is going to answer that question further down in the text.)

Look at verse 18. How does Paul describe the love of Christ?

I love Ephesians 3:17–19 because it is a prayer for others but also for us! I've rewritten these verses in my own prayer below.

Fill in the blanks with the descriptive words you used above to describe the love of Christ, and feel free to use this prayer throughout the week.

Father, please help me be rooted and established in Your love and have the power, together alongside all of Your holy people, to fully grasp and understand just how ______________ and ______________ and ______________ and ______________ is Your love. This love is a love that surpasses all worldly understanding, but God grant me the knowledge to understand it deep in my soul. Amen.

Read Ephesians 4:1–6 and answer the questions below.

What is Paul urging the Ephesians to do (v. 1)?

What does this passage say a life worthy of our calling looks like?

Again, we see a repeating theme from a passage we previously studied. Look up Colossians 1:9–14, and note the similarities below.

What does this passage in Colossians say a life worthy of the Lord looks like?

It's hard to be restless when you understand that your life has a worthy calling. You have a mission right where you are. Your circumstances might shift and change, but your calling as a daughter of Christ will not. And as a result, your life has immense purpose and value, regardless of your circumstances, because you have the knowledge of a saving love that surpasses all understanding. These passages lay out clearly what it means to be rooted and established in love.

Paul's last imperative command for this passage that we're studying is one of unity. Why do you think this was an important repetitive theme in Paul's writings and included as a characteristic of a life worthy of our calling?

As we've discovered, there are many overlapping themes in Ephesians and Colossians. It's believed that the letter to the Colossians was written first, around AD 60–61, and the letter to the Ephesians was written shortly after, around AD 61–62. In its six chapters, the book of Ephesians further develops many of the themes and ideas written in the four-chapter book of Colossians, which is why we see many recurring phrases and themes.

Let's take a closer look at this for today's passage. In the sections below, you'll see some of Paul's recurring ideas in today's passage that are also found in Colossians (we've already compared some of these today, so you've already done the work!).

In the first two columns, you'll see the passages that mirror each other. I've written out the portion in Ephesians that you need to focus on.

In the middle column for Colossians, write out Paul's words. Then in the third column, considering both passages, describe the main idea from these passages.

Paul's words in Ephesians	Paul's words in Colossians	In your own words, what is Paul getting at here?
Ephesians 3:14–16 *For this reason I kneel before the Father . . . I pray that out of his glorious riches he may strengthen you with power through his Spirit.*	**Colossians 1:9**	

Ephesians 3:17 *So that Christ may dwell in your hearts through faith*	**Colossians 3:16**	
Ephesians 3:17 *I pray that you, being rooted and established in love . . .*	**Colossians 2:6–7**	
Ephesians 4:1 *I urge you to live a life worthy of the calling you have received.*	**Colossians 1:10**	
Ephesians 4:2 *Be completely humble and gentle; be patient, bearing with one another in love.*	**Colossians 3:12**	

Ephesians 4:3–4 *Make every effort to keep the unity of the Spirit through the bond of peace. There is one body and one Spirit, just as you were called to one hope when you were called.*	**Colossians 3:15**	
Ephesians 4:5–6 *One Lord, one faith, one baptism; one God and Father of all, who is over all and through all and in all.*	**Colossians 1:16–17**	

I love seeing all the similarities laid out side by side. But this was more than just an exercise to compare and contrast Paul's wording. When ideas and themes are repeated in Scripture, that means they're important. And the main idea for today is that being rooted in the love of Christ instead of restless isn't some fun catchphrase; it's a life-changing, Spirit-led choice that keeps us living lives worthy of our callings.

In light of what you've studied today, what would it look like in your own life to choose to be rooted and established in the love of Christ?

Memory Verse

Read Colossians 3:1–4 and then practice filling in the blanks from memory below.

"____________ ____________, you have ____________ ________________ with ______________, set your ____________ on _____________ ________________, where _____________ is, _______________at the _____________ _____________ of God. ___________ your ________________ on ________________ above, not on _________________ things. For you ___________, and your ____________ is now _________________ with _____________ in _________. When ______________, who is your _________ __________________, then you also will ________________ with ________ in ________________."

Prayer

Feel free to pray this prayer, or write out your own prayer to God below.

God, I'm coming to You today to pray for what Paul prayed for the Ephesians. God, strengthen me with Your power through Your Spirit so that Christ would dwell in my heart through faith. Father, help me be rooted and established in Your love so that, together with all Your holy people, I am able to grasp just how wide and long and high and deep is the love of Christ. Lord, help that knowledge ring true in my heart and mind. In Jesus' name. Amen.

KEY TAKEAWAY: Being rooted instead of restless isn't some fun catchphrase; it's a life-changing, Spirit-led choice that keeps us living lives worthy of our callings.

WEEK 6 | **DAY 4**

No Longer Infants

Ephesians 4:7–32

Spiritual maturity is an interesting concept. It's hard to measure because it doesn't happen naturally with time or age. There are teenagers who have been faithfully walking with Jesus for years, and yet there are adults who are still infants in the faith. Age doesn't necessarily equal maturity in the family of God. Instead, spiritual maturity is measured by who we are becoming more like, day by day.

Are we becoming more like Christ? Or are we still living like our old selves, how we lived prior to knowing the redeeming love of Christ?

Today we are given a clear picture of what spiritual maturity and immaturity are. And I believe it's a fantastic analogy for what it looks like to be rooted in Christ and what it looks like to be restless. This passage of Scripture doesn't pull any punches, but it calls us to a better way of life that is worthy of the calling we learned about yesterday.

Read Ephesians 4:14–19 and answer the questions below.

What name does Paul give a person who is tossed back and forth by the waves?

Which word would you use to describe a person blown here and there by every wind of teaching and by the cunning and craftiness of people in their deceitful scheming? Circle the word.

Rooted ***Restless***

How does Paul describe the people who are deceitfully scheming?

Notice the personal pronoun that Paul is using in verses 14–15. Underline it in your Bible. Write it in all caps below.

This is important. There are many sections of Paul's writings where he uses the plural "you" (hey, y'all!), and it's understood as he's writing to a body of believers. But in these verses, Paul says "we"—including himself!

Why do you think this is an important distinction?

In verse 15, Paul writes:

> *"We will grow to become in every respect the mature body of him who is the head, that is, Christ. From him to the whole body, joined and held together by every supporting ligament, grows and builds itself up in love, as each part does its work."*
> EPHESIANS 4:15

Paul uses "we" because 1) maturation isn't something we do alone; and 2) since we are one body, with many parts, each part has its own work that impacts the rest of the body. Do you see where we're going?

If the church in Ephesus was immature, acting as infants, lured this way and that by every new shiny doctrine, it impacted the whole body of Christ. We (me, you, the apostle Paul included) are called to maturity within the body of Christ, and we each have individual roles that feed into our communal one. We belong to one another, and our maturity (or lack thereof) impacts not just ourselves, but our shared witness and mission!

The point is our maturity isn't just for our good, it's also for the good of the body.

In verse 17–19, Paul encourages the Ephesians to mature and no longer live as the world tells them to.

According to these verses, how do the gentiles (unbelievers) live?

Have you ever given or maybe received the side-eye from a loved one with the admonition, "I know you've been taught better than that"?

In contrast to the previous verses, what do verses 20–24 say about how we should be living?

This may seem impossible—and it is apart from Christ!

But when we put off our old self, we are made new in the "________________________ of your ________________."

Flip to Romans 12:2, and write it below.

With that in mind, is it possible to have a renewed mind apart from Christ?

Ephesians 4:24 call us to "__________ _______ the new self, created to be like God in true righteousness and holiness."

That phrase "put on" is the same one Paul used in Colossians 3:10. Read Colossians 3:10–17. In the space below, list the characteristics we should "put on" or "clothe ourselves" with.

Circle the word below that you would use to describe a person who is clothed in the characteristics above.

Rooted *Restless*

Read Ephesians 4:25–32 for another list of what it looks like to no longer be an infant, but to be a mature Christian who is clothed in righteousness. In these verses, what are some old ways that need to be put off? See if you can find about eight or ten, depending on how you group them.

Again, does this sound like a person who is rooted or a person who is restless?

In the same section, there are some things that we should be doing as mature believers. List them below:

I think you already know which type of Christian this is: *rooted*!

You might be thinking, "Brittany, all of this sounds really good. But I still don't get how this happens. How do I live a godly life, putting off the old self, putting on the new?" And I think that is a fair question.

Look up 2 Peter 1:3–9. According to verse 3, what do we have access to that gives us everything we need for a godly life?

In verses 5–9, we're given another list, a road map of sorts, that describes a life of godliness. The passage states.

> Make every effort to add to your faith ___________________________;
>
> And to goodness, ___________________________;
>
> And to knowledge, ___________________________;
>
> And to self-control, ___________________________;
>
> And to perseverance,___________________________;
>
> And to godliness, ___________________________;
>
> And to mutual affection, _________________.

According to verse 8, if you possess these characteristics in "increasing measure" (meaning you keep growing in them), these are the qualities that keep you from being ___________________________ and ___________________________.

In other words, these are the qualities that help you grow and mature into a believer who is rooted in the knowledge of our Lord Jesus Christ!

As we learned earlier in the study, these lists can easily be used as a measuring stick. They can become a list of dos and don'ts to control or modify our behavior without addressing our hearts! I want to be clear, that is not the gospel and that is not what these passages are saying.

That's why it's important to zoom out a bit and see the context that the second half of Ephesians 4 was written in. Yes, our behavior needs to change, but remember the beginning of chapter 4 that we read yesterday?

What was Paul urging the readers to live? (Hint: look at verse 1.)

Let's look at the beginning of the chapter again to remind ourselves of this context.

Read Ephesians 4:1–13 and answer the questions below.

According to verses 7–13, how are we supposed to accomplish maturity? Is it through our own strength?

Look at the graphic below. Who is doing most of the work here? Fill in the blanks from verses 7–14.

_______________ has given grace and gifts to each of His people (v. 7).

↓

_______________ provided apostles, prophets, evangelists, pastors and teachers to equip the body (v. 11).

↓

These ministers use their gifts to equip the body for acts of service so the body of Christ will be built up in unity in the faith and so that they will become mature (vv. 12–13).

↓

attaining the whole measure of the fullness of _______________ (v. 13).

↓

Then we will no longer be infants (v. 14).

Do you see the chain of events? Who is responsible for giving grace and the gifts to His people?

Who is responsible for providing ministers to equip the body of Christ for acts of service?

This is critical to our spiritual formation, because apart from Christ all of this is behavior modification. Remember what we learned at the beginning of this study: **God is more concerned with who you are becoming than how well you perform for Him.**

A life rooted in Christ, changed by His love, is a force to be reckoned with, not because she performs well but because she is becoming more like Him with each passing day.

It's not simply outward change, but an inward one that that empowers us to be renewed day by day (2 Corinthians 4:16). When we "put on" our new self and clothe ourselves in His righteousness, we become more like Him. He gives us the power to build others up in unity and maturity. What a gift to get to join Him in His work of setting others free from striving and living like unbelievers!

Praise God, in Christ, we have everything we need for a rooted life of godliness.

Memory Verse

Write Colossians 3:1–4 below, and then speak the words aloud three times, working from memory as best as you can. Feel free to use your Bible as needed.

Prayer

Feel free to pray this prayer, or write out your own prayer to God below.

Lord, thank You for Your grace. Thank You for providing Your people with gifts and equipping us to do good works for You, so that we can each play a role in building up the body of Christ. Lord, Your Word tells me that I shouldn't conform to the patterns of this world and that I need to put off my old ways. God, I know that this is all impossible without Your work in my life. God, renew my mind; renew my spirit. Help me to be rooted in Your love so that I don't get tossed back and forth by the waves this world will throw at me. Help me to remember that who I am becoming is more important than attempting to check off a list in order to please You. Your ways are better, and I have everything I need in Christ for a life of godliness. Let this ring true in my heart. In Jesus' name. Amen.

KEY TAKEAWAY: A life rooted in Christ, changed by His love, is a force to be reckoned with, not because she performs well but because she is becoming more like Him with each passing day.

WEEK 6 | DAY 5

Reflection and Wrap-Up

Over the last four days we've learned:

- The philosophies of this world will keep you striving and restless by adding to the work of Jesus. And yet, the good news of Jesus is that He alone saves. He alone is holding all things together. And He alone is reconciling all things in heaven and on earth. So instead of striving, we choose to be rooted and built up in Christ and Christ alone.
- Being rooted instead of restless isn't some fun catchphrase; it's a life-changing, Spirit-led choice that keeps us living lives worthy of our callings.
- A life rooted in Christ, changed by His love, is a force to be reckoned with, not because she performs well but because she is becoming more like Him with each passing day.

Today, I'm going to switch it up a bit. After all, it's our last day together!

Whatever option you chose for this study and whatever journey brought you to this moment, I want you to take a second to celebrate the work you've put in. I also want you to take a moment and celebrate the work that the Lord has done in your heart over the past six weeks.

As a reminder, over the last six sessions we've learned to choose . . .

Relationship instead of Religion (Week 1)
Character instead of Charisma (Week 2)
Service instead of Stages (Week 3)
Community instead of Isolation (Week 4)
Gratitude instead of Grumbling (Week 5)
Rooted instead of Restless (Week 6)

These choices are what will lead us to a life free of striving and performance, firmly rooted in Christ. I'm confident that the time you spent in God's Word has helped your heart find its place in being rooted in Christ rather than striving for anything this world might have to offer.

The questions on our last day are a little different than the previous five weeks. Feel free to also answer our usual batch of questions if you want to reflect on Week 6 more intently. I've included them here for you to reference:

- What is one theme or truth from Scripture that stood out to you the most this week?
- Has anything from this week changed, challenged, or shaped your thinking, your actions, or beliefs? If so, how so?
- What is one idea or verse that has encouraged you that you'd like to carry with you?
- Finish the sentence: Because of Christ, I . . .

But we're going to zoom back out and reflect on the study as a whole on our final day.

Looking back over the last six weeks, which choice have you found to be the most applicable to your life and why?

Is there a passage of Scripture that stood out to you most and why? This passage could have been one that encouraged you, equipped you, or perhaps even convicted you. Write it below, and commit it to memory if you haven't already.

Each day we had a Key Takeaway to summarize what we were learning together. What was your key takeaway from this study as a whole? Write it in your own words below or write it verbatim from the study.

Memory Verse

Write Colossians 3:1–4 from memory below. If you can't, no worries! Grace upon grace! Write it out using your Bible as a reference. But if you can, keep meditating on these so that they will be committed to your long-term memory! Hiding God's Word in our hearts helps us recall His words when we need them most, so great job at sticking with this discipline during this study!

Prayer

We have one final prayer to pray together. And if you'll allow me the honor, I've written a prayer for you on the next page to take with you. It's one that I've prayed over every reader who would open these pages. Feel free to cut it out of this book and tape it to your mirror or put it in a frame by your bed. But use it whenever you feel the pull of striving and performance on your heart.

KEY TAKEAWAY: Rather than solely focus on this week, our key takeaway for the entire study is simply this: **Because of Jesus, we have nothing to prove and nothing to earn.** Praise the Lord!

A Liturgy for the One Who Strives

God of the universe,
You are before all things, and You hold everything together in Your hands.
And yet, You call me beloved and have invited me to a life rooted in Your love.
You have rescued me from darkness, and brought me into the kingdom of light.

And yet, again, I find myself striving.

Striving to earn Your approval, even though it's already been given to me in Christ.
Striving to be seen by others, even though I am seen and loved by You.
Striving to prove my worth through the world's standards,
even though I know Your way is better.

Lord, help me want to become more like You, more than I want to perform for You.
Lord, help me remember that in You I have everything I need for life and godliness.
Lord, help me remember that I am not alone, but have a place in the body of Christ.

And when my heart begins to strive, help me to choose

Relationship instead of Religion
Character instead of Charisma
Service instead of Stages
Community instead of Isolation
Gratitude instead of Grumbling
to be Rooted instead of Restless.

Lord, let it be so of me, of us, and for everyone who reads these words.
In Jesus' holy name,
amen.

APPENDIX

Memory Verses

The memory verses below are listed by week. Feel free to cut them out and use them however you'd like! Tape them to your mirror or hole punch them and put them on a ring to carry with you. Use them however you wish—but they're included as an additional help to you throughout the study!

Week 1: Colossians 3:1

"Since, then, you have been raised with Christ, set your hearts on things above, where Christ is, seated at the right hand of God."

Week 2: Colossians 3:2

"Set your minds on things above, not on earthly things."

Week 3: Colossians 3:1–2

"Since, then, you have been raised with Christ, set your hearts on things above, where Christ is, seated at the right hand of God. Set your minds on things above, not on earthly things."

Week 4: Colossians 3:3

"For you died, and your life is now hidden with Christ in God."

Week 5: Colossians 3:4

"When Christ, who is your life, appears, then you also will appear with him in glory."

Week 6: Colossians 3:1–4

"Since, then, you have been raised with Christ, set your hearts on things above, where Christ is, seated at the right hand of God. Set your minds on things above, not on earthly things. For you died, and your life is now hidden with Christ in God. When Christ, who is your life, appears, then you also will appear with him in glory."

Acknowledgments

Wow! There are so many people who need to be thanked for their work on this book! First and foremost, thank you *Jesus* for the work You've done on the cross and in my own heart! I am so grateful for the opportunity to get to share Your love with others.

Thank you to Ben, my husband and best friend, who can hold the fort down like no other and who is my biggest cheerleader. Thank you for the thousand ways you love me and our kiddos so well.

Speaking of my kids . . . Felicity and Noel, at the time of the writing of this book, you were old enough to understand how important this ministry is to me. Thank you for cheering me on. May you grow into women who have nothing to prove and nothing to earn. Jude and Zeke, there were many afternoons when you two would be wrestling behind me as I typed away at this manuscript in my office. Thank you for the entertainment and for just being you. Eva and Manny, you two were tiny little ones during this book's development. There were many afternoons I was holding one (or both!) of you while typing one-handed. Thank you for the reminder of what is most important in this life.

To the entire team at Moody, thank you. Thank you, Trillia, for first acquiring me and cheering me on. Thank you, Erin, for your constant support and work on this project. Thank you, Amanda, for your careful eye during editing. And to everyone on the design team, the sales team, the marketing team, and many other teams that I don't even know about, I truly am so grateful for every person who contributed to the creation of this project. *Thank you* for your partnership.

To my Writerly Dream Team (you know who you are), thank you for your prayer, for your encouragement, and for the laughs. These friendships were something I didn't expect in this season, but also such a delightful gift from the Lord. Many thanks to each of you. Cheering each of you on in your various ministries.

And lastly, to my local church, Port City Community Church, I adore you. I am grateful for your shepherding and space to grow in my own personal walk with Jesus. Thank you to every staff member and congregant who serves our community faithfully.

Soli Deo Gloria.